the boy on SHADY GROVE ROAD

A CHILDHOOD OF THE 1940s AND 50s IN THE SOUTH

CLYDE McCULLEY

Story Night Press
★ PORTLAND MAINE ★

ACKNOWLEDGEMENTS

There are those whom I wish to thank for their help and understanding as I wrote my childhood memories.

So much appreciation goes to Ann Kimmage, author and retired writing professor, who graciously offered to tutor me as I was writing and encouraged me to continue until the story was finished.

Also a big thank you to Kurt Ganter, an old colleague from our college teaching days who edited the transcript and gave encouragement. Also thanks to Michele Ganter for her reading through the transcripts and helping with the grammar. My dear friend Nancy Greenleaf for offering to give it one last read and made suggestions.

My special thanks goes to my daughter Sheri for the concept and design of the cover and to her husband Tom for his editing suggestions and interior text formatting and page design.

I also want to recognize family members who have encouraged me along the way, my wife Susan for her continued support and encouragement, my daughter Rhonda and her husband Jesse, who reminded me of stories I had told she and Sheri when they were children, my nephews and nieces, Velma, Michael, Lisa, Deborah, Hue, Iris, Ivan, Martha, Sidney and Al and the sweet memories of Howard and Gary Joe.

And to my two step-sons, Jim and Matt, and all the grandkids who complete the package: Justin, Shelby, Austin, Logan, Alice and Benjamin.

Published in the United States by Story Night Press
Portland, Maine
www.storynightpress.com

CONTENTS

INTRODUCTION

I was the last born of six kids into a poor family, in a poor community, on a poor farm with poor soil about three miles from town. My oldest brother, George, was nineteen when I was born. The next youngest to me was my sister, Mary, who was eight years old when I came along.

World War Two was raging and families were rationed food, gas and tires for automobiles by the government. Food was the only thing that affected us since we did not have an automobile. We only had an old farm wagon and two old horses.

As a young child, I did not know we were poor. I had nothing to compare to our lifestyle. I was never hungry or unloved. I thought this was the way people lived.

All I wanted was a little brother to play with. My older sister, Lucy, married and had a baby, Kenny, when I was three years old. He soon grew enough for me to play with. I was his uncle, but to me we were brothers. That was what was important.

Our house was on Shady Grove Road. You can't find it by that name on a county map, because the county had never named it when I was a kid. They just had a number for it on the county map. The neighbors who live on it named it themselves. It was named Shady Grove Road, because at the very end of the road, down by the Little Rock Highway, there was a little gift shop named Shady Grove Gift Shop.

The shop had all kinds of yard ornaments, birdbaths and Chenille bedspreads hanging on lines outside the shop. It also had little junky trinkets that people bought for souvenirs. It was nestled in a shady grove of large pine trees. There was a sign outside that said, "If you can't stop, Honk as you go by." I guess a lot of people liked that, because there was a lot of honking.

So, because of the junky little Shady Grove Gift Shop, we had our own name for our road. I think it is a great name for a road, Shady Grove Road, the road I was born on. It should have been named that on the county map.

I hope that this little Memoir of my formative years, living as The Boy on Shady Grove Road, will give a picture of how important a simple sandy road can be to a small poor boy as he strives to understand the complexities of life.

This is a little book of memories, in little stories, written from the child's viewpoint between the ages of six and twelve years. The stories are not written in an orderly, chronological manner, but rather at random as I remember them. I want the book to be opened to any page and still make sense to the reader without knowing what came before or comes after.

My Beginnings

A little four-room house, a small barn, a few old sheds and an out-house on five acres of poor sandy land half way between Little Rock and Hot Springs, Arkansas was the home place of my beginnings as a child in 1941.

Little House on Shady Grove Road

My Daddy was sixty years old and my mother was forty when I was born in my house, in their bed. Daddy walked to town to get the doctor, but by the time Daddy and the doctor got there, all that was left to do was to circumcise me.

My Daddy married my Momma when he was forty years old and she was only twenty. They met when my mother visited her half brother, Marvin, in Memphis, Tennessee. Uncle Marvin lived next door to my father and his mom and dad. They had a nice house, nice furniture and five children, George, Willy, Lucy, Sue and Mary.

Daddy worked for the Otis Elevator Company as a mechanic. During the 1930s my father lost his job with the elevator company. Nobody ever talked about why my Daddy lost his job. I wondered, but never asked.

He had saved some money and the family lived on it until it was almost gone. In 1938 Daddy moved the family to a small rural community of Congo, Arkansas, about eight miles from Benton, the county seat, to try to make a living. My Momma's half-sister, Ola, and her husband Judd lived near there and it was the reason they settled in the area. They moved their good furniture with them. He found cheap land and tried to farm it. It was quite rocky and did not produce.

He later decided they needed to move to another place, perhaps to a place with better soil.

He moved Momma and their five kids to the house on Shady Grove Road in 1940. Daddy paid five hundred dollars for the four-room house, one small barn, a chicken house, a shed and an outdoor toilet. It sat on five acres of sandy land.

Shady Grove Road was a small dirt road. The house was near the corner of Congo Road, which was gravel. The house was three miles from town. It had no electricity or running water. Daddy did not have a car, only two skinny old horses, Smoky and Dan, an old cow named Cow and a wagon. Most of the people on our road were poor and with little education. The Depression had been hard and many never seemed to recover.

President Roosevelt was trying to help the poor with some of his new programs. He had a big job on his hands. My Daddy would not accept the welfare money the President offered the poor. Pride, I guess.

When I was born in 1941, there were now six kids, with George, the oldest. He was 19 years old and immediately joined the Marines. The next oldest, Willy, went to work in Mr. Roosevelt's Civilian Conservation Corps camps until he was old enough to join the Navy. They both knew there were too many mouths to feed on the small amount of money the little dirt farm produced.

Mary, the closest to me in age, was eight years older. Now there were only Daddy and Momma and three girls and me to live in our four rooms and an outdoor toilet.

Before I was born, my Momma had converted to the religion of which my Aunt Ola was a member. It was The Seventh-day Adventist. The church services were held on Saturday and it followed the teachings of the Old Testament Bible and was very conservative. There was no dancing, no movies, no working on the Saturday Sabbath from sundown Friday to sundown Saturday, no pork or shellfish, no coffee, no jewelry and of course smoking and alcohol were considered a sin.

My Daddy did not believe in belonging to any church. He considered it a waste of time.

He said most Christians were hypocrites, so my childhood years were spent going to church with my Momma and drinking coffee and eating bacon with my Daddy.

When I was six years old, I said to my Daddy, "We are poor." He glared at me and said, "We are not poor, we are just a little short on money." Then he said, "The Johnsons, who live down Shady Grove Road, are poor. Their kids only have white bread with mustard and sugar for sandwiches most of the time. We have baloney sandwiches, so don't ever think of us as poor."

My Momma did not have a job outside the house.

We lived in a four-room house that had been a dance hall before my family bought it. There was a two-holer outhouse with a door. The smaller hole was for kids, and the larger hole for adults. Some neighbors only had a one-holer outhouse. We obviously were not poor, only a little short on money.

Both of my brothers saw it their duty to send money back home from the service to help the family. My oldest sister, Lucy, left home to try to make it on her own. She later met a man 15 years older. She married and had a baby named Kenneth Jr., after his Daddy.

Times were tough for our family and for the nation, which was engrossed in war. Everyone had his or her own problems to deal with and I was waiting for Kenny to get older so I would have a "brother" to play with.

Kenny is Born

I was three years old when Kenny was born. This was my first memory as a child. Lucy and Kenneth Sr. lived in Hot Springs. It was twenty miles from our house. Momma and I took the Greyhound Bus to see the new baby. Lucy lived in an apartment house, something I did not know anything about. Other strange people lived in the same house. I was not so sure about this kind of living.

Lucy had already brought the baby home by the time we arrived. Kenny was born in a hospital, not in his Momma and Daddy's bed like me.

It was raining hard–"Raining cats and dogs," Momma said. I wondered why I could not see dogs and cats. I stood by the metal screen door watching the rain hit the street. There was lots of lightning and thunder. I loved both. Momma yelled at me "You are going to be struck by lighting if you stay by that metal door." So I moved back a little. Still there were no cats or dogs. I think she was teasing me.

I was very happy about Kenny. Now I had a brother to grow up with. Momma explained that he was not really my brother, but to me he was.

When Momma and I returned home on the bus Daddy had a frown on his face. The big storm had blown away our chicken house with the chickens in it. We only had six chickens. They were dead and lying all over the field. So we ate chicken all week. The baloney had to wait for another time. But now there were no eggs. Daddy had to buy more chickens.

Daddy gave Lucy and Kenneth Sr. a little piece of our land. They built a small house on it. Kenny was only a baby. Now he was close by and I visited a lot. I wanted him to grow fast so we could play together.

Kenneth Sr. got a job in town working on jukeboxes and pinball machines. Now they had a little money, but they still ate baloney sandwiches.

Triangle Café

I was six years old when I ate my first meal ever in a restaurant. Kenny, his Momma and Daddy took me to The Triangle Café in town. There was a wonderful smell coming from the greasy grill. I asked for a hamburger with pickles, onions and mustard. Kenny was only three years old and he said he wanted a hamburger without onions.

As we sat there, the beautiful Coca Cola neon sign fascinated me. I loved the way the colors glowed. There were several booths with other people in them. They, too, were eating hamburgers. A jukebox stood in the corner. The jukebox was playing Hank Williams records. I decided right then that I always wanted to eat Triangle hamburgers and learn to sing like Hank Williams.

After that, I always liked hamburgers and I sang a lot like Hank until I turned twelve, when my voice changed and I lost my ability to sing, but a lot of other exciting things happen to a boy when he turns twelve.

Saturday Night Bath

Most houses on Shady Grove Road did not have running water unless you ran to the well to get it. We did not have an indoor bathroom like a few of the people who lived further up the Congo Road or the people in town with money.

Momma would put a kettle of water on the kerosene stove and heat it. Then she would pour hot water and then cold water into our galvanized laundry tub in the kitchen and have me climb in.

It was a round tub and only had room to sit in it if you pulled your legs uptight. Momma would have me stand up in the tub and then pour water over me to rinse off the soap. This would happen once a week, whether I needed it or not. In cold weather the bath had to be taken in the living room next to the pot-belly wood stove.

When I was in second grade my Momma started doing housework for a doctor in town. He lived in a nice part of town. Some of the houses in his neighborhood were made of brick.

One day my Momma told me to walk over to the doctor's house after school. When I got there the doctor and his wife were not home. Momma said she had a surprise for me. She took me into the bathroom and there was a big long white bathtub. She ran the tub about half full with warm water and told me to get in.

I could not believe it. I had swum in rivers and lakes, but had never been in a tub of warm water before. I was able to stretch out and pretend to be swimming. I went under water and held my breath.

I decided right then and there that I did not want to be poor, or be a person without money. I wanted what rich people had, a long white bathtub with warm water.

Modern Living

One day when I got home from school, there were some big trucks on Shady Grove Road in front of my house. Men were digging deep holes with very long-handled shovels.

I asked them what they were digging for. "We are here to put in electric poles to bring electricity to your house," they said. I was very excited. This would almost be like living in town.

The next day a man came into our house to put in electric wires. My Daddy told him to put one outlet in each of our four rooms and hang a light down from the ceiling in each room. The man said that we might need more than one outlet in each room. My Daddy said, "I don't think so. We will only have an electric radio and possibly an electric iron. What would we ever do with the other plugs?"

A few days later they turned on the electricity. It was just like being at my Aunt Ola's house. (She had had electricity for about two years.) At night you could see in every corner of the rooms. You could read without hurting your eyes. But still when I colored with crayons at night, yellow still did not show up very well. I realized that electricity could not fix everything.

Daddy had been trying to save a little money for these modern things. The year before he knew they were going to put in the poles for the electricity, he had men install a propane gas tank in our yard. Instead of having a potbelly wood stove in the living room to heat the house, we now had two little gas heaters, one heater for the living room, and one for the two bedrooms. Daddy also bought a gas refrigerator. I could not understand how burning gas could make ice, but it did.

This meant that the iceman would not be coming to our house every week. I loved it when he brought ice. Momma would put an "Ice card" in our front window that would show the iceman how much ice we wanted. There were several numbers: 25, 50, 75 and 100. The iceman could read from his truck the number at the top, showing him how large a chunk of ice she wanted that week. The iceman would take an ice pick and chop away the size chunk she wanted from a huge block in the back of his truck. He always chopped off a small piece of ice for me. It was like a Popsicle, but no flavor. It was great anyway.

Daddy told me to help him haul the old wood oak icebox down to the ditch behind our house. We did not need that old thing anymore. We were getting modern.

But now I missed the iceman coming each week and giving me my chunk of ice.

FAMILY LIFE

I came along eight years after Momma and Daddy thought they were through having kids.

We were poor, dirt poor as they say, but I remember joy in my childhood with my family. We listened to the radio, my parents read children's books to me, my Father carved wooden whistles out of hickory tree limbs and they allowed Kenny and me the freedom to be adventurous all summer, barefoot and alone by ourselves in the fields and woods.

My father said, "We are not poor, we are just a little short on money." I appreciate, to this day, his optimistic nature, even when times got really hard.

We still loved, talked, listened and ate all of our meals together. It was special.

My Momma, Bless Her Little ol' Heart

Bless his little ol' heart, or Bless her little ol' heart. That's what my Momma would say about people. It could have many different meanings, from *"I think she is terrific and she deserves it,"* to *"poor thing, she should have known better."*

I have heard Momma only say two bad things in my life. One day, when she fell and hurt her leg, she said, "Shit Fire, and Save the Matches", which I thought had some merit. Another time, she said, "I don't know whether to Shit or go Blind." I did not understand this, as I was hoping to someday be an artist and being blind would not be a benefit.

My Momma was simple, loving and hardworking. She was the only child of her Momma and Daddy. Her Momma had been married before and had several children (including Aunt Ola and Uncle Marvin) before her first husband's early death.

When my Momma was only six years old, she lost both parents due to illnesses. She was sent to live with her momma's sister, Aunt Hilda in Lake City, Arkansas, near Jonesboro.

She never went to high school, but went to work instead, as many young girls did in those days.

A few years later, she was visiting her older half brother, Marvin, at his home in Memphis, when she met my Daddy. Daddy lived with his parents in their home next door to Marvin. They fell for each other. Daddy had been a bachelor until he met my Momma. That was it. He was forty and she was twenty, but neither seemed concerned. They would make it work.

They married and had five kids. Things were great for about fifteen years. They had a nice home, nice furniture and a nice car. Daddy was a mechanic at the Otis Elevator Company. After that he lost his job. They lived on their savings for a while, then had to sell their house.

In 1938, the savings were gone and out of desperation they moved the kids and furniture to the Congo community, which was out in the country in Arkansas, to try to farm. It did not work.

Later they moved closer to town, to Shady Grove Road, where I was born. Things did not improve.

My Momma had to adjust to a hard life, trying to raise six kids in a house with no electricity, no running water and no indoor plumbing and a husband without a job. Daddy tried to do a little truck farming, basically to raise food to "put-up" for the winter.

As I got a bit older, I tried to help her wash the clothes. We had to carry the water from the well. She would build a wood fire under a big black pot in the yard to boil water. Then, she would pour the hot water into the hand-operated washer. I would take the handle and slosh the water back and forth to get the dirt out of the clothes. Then I would run them through a hand wringer to remove as much water as possible. Then they had to be rinsed. When we rinsed the white clothes, Momma would put Mrs. Stewart's Bluing in the rinse. She said by adding the bluing, it made the whites look whiter. It was magic to me.

I would help her hang the clothes on the clothesline. Washing clothes was an all day affair. She always tried to be through with the washing in time to listen to her favorite soap opera, *Stella Dallas*, on the radio at 4:00 pm. It was one of the simple joys in her life. The other was reading the Bible. It gave her some hope, I think. It was the only book I ever saw her read, except for the children's books she read to me.

She would tell me that she wanted me to go through High School and maybe even to one of those colleges. She said she was pretty sure they would teach art there.

I promised her I would. She was good to me, loving and kind, and I wanted to do that for her. She was a sweet person who cared.

Summer Rain Coming

In summer we could smell the rain coming. The thunder rolled like a big log truck coming down the Congo Road. You could smell the scent of dirt as the rain pounded the plowed fields nearby. The wind of the storm blew the wet earth smell to us. Daddy looked at the sky and said, "It is going to rain cats and dogs." It never did.

When the storm hit, there was a funnel cloud above us. It did not touch down, though. But it did rain small frogs all over our front yard. They were jumping everywhere. Daddy said, "The funnel cloud pulled them up out of the swamp a few miles away and dropped them on our front yard."

Cats and dogs had better stay away from the swamp unless they want to make my Daddy's sayings come true for a change.

Nighttime Radio

Before we got electricity, we had a radio that was powered by a battery. The battery was larger than the radio. When we had electricity installed in our house we also got a new smaller radio that didn't need a battery.

Country people depended on the radio for news, weather, the price of hogs and cotton as well as for entertainment. In the afternoon there were stories on the radio called soap operas. That's when Momma would iron clothes and listen to her favorite show at 4:00, the Stella Dallas Show.

In the evenings we listened to detective stories like Dragnet and Dr. King, Private Eye. On Saturday nights, we could pick up WSM, the big Nashville station many miles away, and listen to the *Grand Ole Opry*.

In the summertime, Daddy would place the radio near the window so we could sit outside in the yard and listen. It was cooler outside at night. We listened and imagined the stories we were hearing. We would all sit in a circle in the pitch dark on cool metal lawn chairs.

We sweated and fanned ourselves with paper fans that had a picture of Jesus on them. We got them from the Ashby Funeral Home when we attended the funeral of our young neighbor, Frank Paulson. He was killed in a tragic accident at work for the Alcoa Aluminum Company. He drove a big Euk dump truck. It slid over the edge of the road and down into the mine.

We listened to thrillers and scary radio shows. *The Shadow Knows* and the sound of the screeching door on *The Inner Sanctum Mysteries* were favorites. We would get goose bumps on our arms so big that even the mosquitoes would leave us alone.

During the radio shows, no one would say a word. We just listened. At the end of the evening Momma would say, "Everybody to bed." Again, no one would say anything.

I would just get up and go around to the side of the house to take a pee and then go in the house and crawl into my bed.

It had been a good evening. We had all sat together, in a circle, in the dark and listened and imagined stories. It worked for us.

Saturday Night in Town

Uncle Judd and Aunt Ola would come by our house on Saturday evening and take Momma and me to town with them. This was always special for us, getting to see the main square of town all lit up. All the stores were open, which gave the working people a chance to buy things they needed. They would all close at 5:00 during weekdays.

Uncle Judd and I were ready to get out of the car as soon as we parked on the main square, but it was not yet sundown at the end of the Adventist Sabbath. Momma and Aunt Ola would say, "Why don't we just sit and watch the people walk around the block for a while." Uncle Judd and I knew that they were waiting until the exact moment the sun went down and the Sabbath day would have ended.

Aunt Ola checked her watch every few minutes and finally said; "The Sabbath is past so we can now get out and go see what is new in the stores. We have followed the letter of the law according to the Bible."

There were only a few stores that I wanted to go into. One was Gingle's Shoe Store. I could put my feet into the wonderful Fluoroscope x-ray machine and see the bones in my feet. Uncle Judd liked this too, so he went with me. Momma and Aunt Ola did not enjoy this thing that we thought was marvelous.

Momma and Aunt Ola went into dress shops. I think Momma wanted to go in to see the latest style of dresses. Then, she could go home and make herself a dress out of her new printed feed sack on her Singer Sewing machine. Aunt Ola could afford to buy herself one, and she usually did.

Uncle Judd also went with me to the Oklahoma Tire and Supply Store, which sold a lot of bicycles and tires for cars and trucks, as well as a lot of other great things. I loved the smell of rubber when we walked in the door. It meant new bicycles to me. I looked at the beautiful bikes and hoped that one day I would have one.

Eventually we all returned to the car and headed home. Uncle Judd said he had a surprise for us. Soon he pulled the car into the parking lot of a brand new brightly lit store. The sign on top said, "Dairy Queen." Uncle Judd said, "They just opened. We have to try out this new type of ice cream." Boy, did that sound good to me.

We all got out of the car and walked to the line of people waiting to get up to the little window where they take your order.

We read the sign:

Cones: Small –5 cents, Large–10 cents
Sundaes: 15 cents–Chocolate, Strawberry, Pineapple
Milk Shakes: 20 cents, with Malt 25 cents

I asked Uncle Judd which I could have. He said, "Since this is new to us, I think we should all get a Sundae." I had never eaten a Sundae before, but I was ready.

I asked for a Pineapple Sundae. I loved Pineapple. The ice cream came out of a machine. He did not have to dip the ice cream out of a container. He just turned a handle and ice cream filled the Sundae cup. This was something new. I was thrilled.

We all stood in front of the Dairy Queen and ate our Sundaes. The ice cream was so smooth. Uncle Judd said, "From now on we will only buy the nickel cones." I guess he needed to save his money for the peanut brittle candy he loved so much. A nickel cone was just fine with me.

I could not wait to get home and tell Kenny about this new discovery. We will pick up cold drink bottles, sell them to Mr. Lacky at his store, then ride our bikes to the Dairy Queen and get one of these fabulous ice cream cones.

Uncle Marvin and Aunt Madeline's Visit

Uncle Marvin was Momma's older half brother. Aunt Madeline was a woman and a half. She was short and almost as wide as she was tall. I loved Uncle Marvin. I tolerated Aunt Madeline.

They were from Memphis, about a three-hour drive from our house on Shady Grove Road. They lived in town where there were sidewalks and the city picked up the garbage. They didn't have to burn their trash in an old oil drum like we did.

They always stopped and visited us each year on their way to Hot Springs. Uncle Marvin believed that the hot baths in the big bathhouses would do his arthritis a lot of good. He also had a small collapsible tin cup that he used for drinking the free hot water that flowed from the public drinking fountains up and down the main street in Hot Springs. He always let me play with his tin cup when he came to see us.

Uncle Marvin was tall and he wore an old-fashioned hearing aid with a little microphone on the end of a wire that stuck out between the buttons on his shirt. The other end of the wire ran to his hearing aid in his left ear. The microphone was right at my height so I could speak right in front of him and he could hear me clearly. Aunt Madeline was short. When she spoke she sounded like a little yapping dog.

Uncle Marvin had a hearing aid and Aunt Madeline had a black hair growing out of a mole right on the point of her chin. It was right at my height too.

When they first arrived, Uncle Marvin shook hands with me as I spoke into his microphone. Aunt Madeline opened her arms and gave me a big hug. Aunt Madeline had huge bosoms. She pulled me into them until my nose was between them and my eyes were staring straight into the big black hair growing out of the big mole on her big pointed chin. That was not a funny thing. She always had a strange smell. I didn't know if this was bosom smell or if her whole body smelled that way. I didn't want to know.

Aunt Madeline had a little problem adjusting to our humble house on Shady Grove Road. We all drank out of a bucket of water since we didn't have running water in the house. We all used the same dipper with a long handle. We took a drink from the dipper, then put it back in the bucket. She almost gagged. She always used Uncle Marvin's folding tin cup to dip down in the bucket for her drink.

She also brought her own roll of toilet paper with her from Memphis. She did not like to use our catalog as toilet paper. I knew by the look on her face when she came out of the outhouse that she wished she had just found herself a bush instead.

I thought they sort of felt sorry for us, them being from the big city and having money and indoor toilets.

They always brought us little gifts, which I both loved and hated because Momma always said, "Now give Aunt Madeline a big hug and thank her." So I had to hold my breath and had my face pulled into those smelly big bosoms and stare straight at the big black hair growing out of that big ugly mole. I loved the gift but I could not say thank you because I couldn't breathe.

They never spend the night with us, only a few hours during the day. I thought only one trip to our outhouse per visit was all she could take.

After the visit was over and they left, Momma said, "Now wasn't that nice of Aunt Madeline to bring you those nice little gifts?" I just looked at Momma and took a big breath. Then I went to the back porch and poured some water in the washbasin and tried to wash the Aunt Madeline smell off me, and off the toys she brought.

Sometimes gifts were not always worth it.

A Frown on Daddy's Face

From as long as I could remember Daddy always had a frown on his face. It was permanent. It had grown there over the years, I thought to myself.

One day I asked him if he was happy. He answered, Yes, I am happy. I have your Momma, six kids, a son-in-law, and a grandson. I am sure that George, Willy, Betty Sue, and Mary Louise will get married someday and give me more grandkids. "Oh, yes," he said, "And someday you will marry too." I just laughed. Then he went on, "We also own our little house, with no liens on it, a garden to grow our food, two old horses with a wagon, a cow and a dozen chickens and a very good rooster." (I was not sure what he meant by "a very good" rooster).

He said he wished that he had not gotten a hernia years ago because it made it hard for him to work or to get work, especially at his age. He said he missed working and it would help the family if he had money coming in.

He told me he quit school when he was twelve years old and started working in a grocery store. When he was sixteen he was hired as an elevator mechanic in Memphis. He saved money by living as cheap as he could. He said the only thing he splurged on was a little beer now and then, but no money on women.

When he was twenty-five years old he heard they were discovering new oil in Oklahoma and everyone that drilled was making money. He decided that he would buy the rights to drill for oil. He said he paid a lot of money for the land lease and rights to drill, plus the money the drilling company charged him. They drilled and drilled, but his leased land did not produce oil. He was heartbroken. He said the money lost was a very large amount and in those days he could have bought a number of brand new cars for the amount of money he lost.

He had been saving every penny he had in order to invest. Now it was all gone. He moved back to the house of his parents in Memphis and continued to work as a mechanic for the Otis Elevator Company, paid this parents a little rent and went back to saving again. His parents died a few years later and then the house became his. He continued to save his money.

His house was next door to Marvin and Madeline Williams, my Momma's half brother and his wife. It was there that he met my Momma and they were married. She was twenty and he was forty. They lived comfortably, had a nice car, and five kids. Then Daddy was injured and later lost his job in the late 30s. That was when they moved to Arkansas. Life did not go very well after the move.

Daddy told me that he refused to think of the family as poor. He and Momma had made up their minds to just make the best of the hard times they were having. He said, "Then you were born, and Momma joined Aunt Ola's church." He said joining the church seemed to help her in spirit, but he could never see that a church would do him any good. He did not trust preachers. He never did tell me why.

Then he asked me if I was happy. He said he knew that I did not always have what some of the other kids had. I said, "Oh, Daddy, I am very happy. We have neighbors who have less than we do. I also know kids at public school that have holes in their overalls and their shoes are worn out. I have toys and other play-pretties. We have a lot of things that others don't, and most of all, we have a good family." He smiled at me. I was glad to see the frown leave his face for a little while, even though I knew it would return. It had grown there for a long time.

New Christmas Tree Lights

One Christmas our tree was covered with the most beautiful colored electric lights. It was another new gift from Aunt Madeline.

The lights looked like little candles. There were small bubbles that went from the bottom to the top of each glass tube. They kept bubbling and bubbling. It was unbelievable. It added so much to our tree. I sat on the floor and gazed at the lights for hours. They made our little house so beautiful.

We got some Angel Hair to put on the tree. Someone said it was made of fiberglass. All I knew was that it made you itch if you got it on your hands and arms. It was beautiful, though.

We hung the icicles on the tree. I think they were made out of tin foil, and we added roping made of red cellophane. We had heard that people make fake snow for the tree out of soap that comes in a box. It was called Ivory Flakes.

So Momma bought a box. We mixed the flakes in a bowl with warm water. It got thick, and we coated each branch of the cedar tree. It did look like snow.

Our tree was just wonderful. If Santa could not work it out to bring us gifts this year, then our beautiful tree would be enough. I loved Christmas.

A few nuts and oranges and ribbon candy would be nice, though.

Momma's Home Cookin'

Early one Sunday morning Momma asked me to go to the edge of the woods to pick some Polk salad greens for supper. She said the greens were more tender if picked when the dew was still on them. She had explained to me before that Polk greens were the first part of the Polk Berry bush to shoot out of the ground when it started to grow each spring. When well cooked, the new leaves could be eaten until they grew to be about eight inches tall. Momma said after that you should not pick them to eat because the bush becomes poisonous. Deep purple berries grew on the bush when it got about as tall as Kenny and me. We picked and smashed the berries to make purple ink out of them. The birds ate the berries and did not die, but they had bird stomachs, and Kenny and I knew we should not eat them.

I went down the path to Kenny's house and woke him up. I told him to come along and help me pick Polk greens.

We went down near the muscadine grapevine where there were lots of Polk greens. We picked a sack full and headed back up to the house and gave them to Momma.

She was happy and asked us if we would like for her to fry us an apple pie for breakfast. We loved her fried apple pies. We said, "Yes, and put lots of cinnamon, sugar and butter in them, please."

She made two half-moon shaped pies for each of us. She poured me a cup of black coffee and Kenny a glass of sweet milk, fresh from our old cow named Cow. (Kenny did not like black coffee. My Daddy had said that black was the only way to drink it, but Kenny always chose milk.) We sat down and enjoyed a wonderful breakfast.

While Momma was cleaning and doing other things, we ate our pies and talked about all the great things she cooked for us. In addition to fried apple pies, we also loved bacon and eggs (Kenny wanted his eggs scrambled), biscuits with white flour gravy poured on top, and of course more biscuits to split open for lots of butter and homemade jelly or jam or preserves.

Dinner at noontime was usually sandwiches and a bowl of homemade soup and cornbread with sweet milk or sour milk (home-churned buttermilk). Sometimes we had sweet tea or Kool Aid as a treat.

For supper Momma often made fried potatoes and poured white flour gravy over the top. We both loved that. We also had cornbread (I liked to break mine up in my sweet milk and eat it with a spoon), fried okra, navy or pinto beans and some type of cooked greens (spinach, turnip, Polk, collards; always with vinegar poured over them).

Momma always believed, as did many southern mommas, that you had to cook your food to death in order for it to be healthy.

We hardly ever ate raw vegetables as part of our meals except for onions, the little kind with the green tops, which Kenny and I sometimes used like straws to suck our milk from the glass. Daddy would sometimes eat little green raw hot peppers that he called "hotter en' hell bullets." Kenny and I tried one of the hot "bullets." We cut it in half, touched it to our lips and almost burned them off. We gave the "bullet" back to Daddy. He almost died laughing. We did not laugh with him.

Sometimes Momma saved a little money and bought minute steaks at the Stewarts' grocery store. That was the least expensive steak she could buy.

She would get out her chopping board and lay the thin steaks on it. With the edge of a saucer she would pound the steaks until they were tender enough for us to chew. She would fry them in the iron skillet until well done, put them on our plates and pour white flour gravy over them. White flour gravy made everything taste wonderful.

She always tried to have some kind of dessert; sometimes banana pudding made with vanilla wafers, home-made cookies, coconut or lemon meringue pies and, every now and then, a pineapple upside-down cake that she made in her iron skillet (this was my absolute favorite).

She made southern fried chicken only for special occasions, like birthdays, Thanksgiving, Christmas or when Aunt Madeline and Uncle Marvin from Memphis came to visit.

After a while, Momma came to the table and asked what we wanted for supper with our Polk salad. I said, "I cannot think of anything more wonderful than fried potatoes with white flour gravy, fried okra, cornbread and banana pudding and sweet tea. Those are the things growing boys need to make them strong and good looking." Kenny laughed.

She said, "Good, now how about you boys doing the dishes for me?" We grinned and said we would be happy too.

Working for Uncle Judd

When I was eleven years old Uncle Judd pulled into our yard in a brand-new green 1952 Chevrolet pickup truck. I could not believe it. I had never known anyone who bought new cars, only older used ones. He was grinning from ear to ear, showing all his snaggled teeth (he had almost every-other tooth missing). "How do you like my new pickup, Clydie," he said. "Get in and we will go to the store and buy us some candy."

At the store we sat on the tailgate of the new truck and ate our candy. Uncle Judd told me that he would like to have me do some work for him at his sawmill.

He said that he got a bunch of saws and wood lathes from a mill near Memphis. The mill had burned and he bought all of the burned equipment. He wanted me to clean and repaint the machinery he had purchased. He would pay me twenty-five cents an hour plus have Aunt Ola fix lunch for me each day. He said she would also have graham crackers and a Dr. Pepper for me at 10:00, 2:00, and 4:00, all for free.

Daddy had told me that I should always "keep an eye on" not only what Uncle Judd said, but also what he "didn't say." I was not sure what Daddy meant by that, but I remembered it.

I told him I would work for him. Then he took me to the Dairy Queen and bought a large ice cream cone for me, something he never did.

I arrived Monday morning and he came out of the house and handed me a cup of hot coffee. He knew I liked coffee. He gave me a steel-wire brush, sand paper, a gallon of battleship grey paint and a paintbrush. He said, "I want you to clean and paint them to look like they have never been in a fire." I asked him if the fire had done damage to more than just the looks of the machines. He said, "I am sure that there was no damage, but no one questions if things look good." He gave me a big grin showing his snaggled teeth.

Then he told me something he said I was always to remember: *"I bought that paint at Gingle's Hardware for two dollars a gallon, but when you paint it on the machinery, it is worth a hundred dollars a gallon."* He asked me if I understood. I said, "Yes."

I did not tell Uncle Judd, but I was starting to understand what Daddy meant by "keeping an eye" on him.

I spent two weeks cleaning and painting until the machinery all looked like new. Uncle Judd had a big sale, sold it all and made a lot of money. I did not make as much, only two dollars per day, but I did enjoy lunch, three Dr. Peppers and graham crackers that I shared with Aunt Ola each day. But as Daddy had suggested, each day I wrote down my hours and made sure that I had received what I had coming. I "kept my eye" on him.

Home Remedies

Daddy turned sixty-eight years old. To my knowledge he had never gone to a doctor. He said his only problem was some arthritis in his fingers and that *prostrate* thing he had. I was not sure I understood what a *prostrate* did exactly.

He wore a truss, an awkward thing that he had to wear around his belly for his hernia. He got the hernia from lifting something too heavy. He said the truss kept his guts from spilling out.

He did not take any medicines from a doctor. He said they were worthless. He did believe in Carter's Little Liver Pills, which he took faithfully along with Geritol and Sloan's Liniment for his sore fingers.

He used Campho-Phenique oil ointment on what he called skin cancer on his face. Fricky Johnson said she thought they were just old age spots. He also used some of his home remedies on me. If a bee or wasp stung me, he would take snuff from his lower lip and dab it on my sting. It took the swelling and pain away. It worked every time.

If I got a cough or sore throat, he took a spoon full of sugar and added two or three drops of Kerosene to it and had me swallow it. "The sugar helps you swallow it" he said "and the Kerosene oils your cords. It makes you feel better, like a well oiled machine."

I never wanted to complain about having a stomachache because both Momma and Daddy believed in castor oil. It was terrible-tasting stuff, but they insisted and I usually threw up right after taking it, which usually got me over my stomachache. So I guess it did work.

Daddy said he was healthy because of the food he ate. He drank his coffee black, wanted biscuits daily, and loved grease. He had my Momma fry pork chops for him, and then had her pour all the grease from the frying pan over his plate of food. He sopped the grease with his biscuit. He said it kept him well lubricated.

My Momma did not drink coffee, did not eat pork, cooked her vegetables to death and went to the doctor and took bunches of different pills.

I thought maybe I should drink black coffee, eat pork and drink grease. I wanted to be healthy. I did eat white Wonder Bread for lunch. The advertisement said it "builds strong bodies eight ways."

Strange they never told us what the "eight ways" were.

Gophers and an Accident

In the summertime Momma always let me go barefoot from the time school was out for the summer until school started again in the fall. I loved going barefoot. The first day I stepped on the new spring grass, it seemed that a wonderful thrill went through my body. The bottom of my feet got pretty tough after a week or so after I began going without shoes.

It was Sunday. I was in the yard playing by myself. Kenny was at his house. His mother did not have to work on Sundays, so he stayed with her.

We had a lot of gophers in our yard. They would make tunnels just below the surface. They would push the ground up and you could see where they tunneled.

Daddy hated them. He bought a tool that looked like it had four sharp knives, or spades on the bottom of it. It also had a spring. It was made to push into the ground. If a gopher went under the tool, the animal would trigger it. The spring would release the four knives and they would slice through the ground and hopefully into the gopher, killing it.

We pushed the tool into the ground in a number of places in the yard, but we never seemed to kill a gopher. I think they were too smart.

I found the spade tool fascinating and played with it, although Daddy had told me not to. I started stabbing the gopher killer tool into the ground, just for fun. I started walking and stabbing. As I walked around the corner of the house, Momma called for me to come in for supper. I looked up for a moment. I jabbed the spiked tool down once more and it went right through my foot, right between my pinky and next toe on my right foot.

I started screaming for Momma. I tried to run to her. The spear was still in my foot as I ran.

She came running out and nearly fainted when she saw it. She held me and gently pulled out the spear. I cried like crazy. She took me into the house, and sat me on a chair. She looked at the wound. One of the four spears had gone completely through my foot. It was bleeding both top and bottom.

She heated some water in the teakettle and started to bathe my foot. After washing away the blood, she told me that she needed to try to get the germs out of the wound. The problem was that the hole went all the way through.

She said, "I am going to get the bottle of hydrogen peroxide and we will try to pour it through the wound." She pressed the bottle upside down against my foot and held it there. She said, "We will have to hold it here for a while, until the Peroxide goes all the way through the wound." She told me to be watching for little foaming bubbles to come out the bottom of my foot. This helped take my mind off the horrible pain I was suffering.

In a few minutes, we started to see little bubbles foaming on the bottom of my foot. She continued to hold the bottle to my foot for a bit longer. "Now," she said. "I think we have cleared any germs that might have gotten into your foot." I stopped crying.

Daddy came home from town just as we finished. He looked at my foot and said he needed to put a piece of chewed tobacco on it. Momma said she did not think so. She thought the Peroxide would do the job.

I lived. It did not get infected and in a few days I was running around the yard again. My foot was still sore.

I was really glad that Daddy had never been successful in killing a gopher with the tool. I would not want to live the rest of my life with a small piece of gopher meat inside my foot.

Aunt Lil

As a child, I had heard the name Aunt Lil, but I had never met her and really did not know anything about her, except she was Momma's half sister. Aunt Ola and Aunt Lil had a different daddy than my Momma, but all three women had the same momma.

I would sometimes overhear Momma and Daddy talking about Aunt Lil, but they would stop talking when I entered the room. I tried to ask Aunt Ola to tell me about Aunt Lil, but she only changed the subject and told me to go play in the attic.

Daddy had a few rows of grapevines growing in the field near Shady Grove Road close to an old shed where Kenny and I liked to play. We would pick a few bunches of grapes, then go inside the shed and make believe that it was our clubhouse.

Momma was home. Daddy had walked to town. Kenny and I spent the morning swimming in Gerard's pond and had come home for dinner at 12:00 sharp, like Momma had told us to do.

When we came into the house to eat, Momma seemed upset and very nervous. Kenny and I looked at each other. We knew something was really wrong. I asked Momma what it was that upset her. She did not want to say. I asked her if someone was dead, or had been killed.

She said, "No, nothing like that." I said, "Please tell us then." She just said she had to think about what to do.

After we ate, we headed out the back door to go back to the pond. I said, "Kenny lets go play in the grape vineyard." I wanted to stay near the house because Momma was acting so strange.

We went to the little vineyard and picked grapes as we had many times before. We started to go into our clubhouse in the shed. I put my hand on the door handle. Just as I started to pull the door open we heard a woman's horrifying scream, then crying coming from the shed. We both froze in our tracks. We could not move, we were both scared to death. Kenny grabbed me and held on for dear life. I told him to let go and I would open the door a little to see what on earth was happening. He begged me not to open the door, but the woman, whoever she was, was crying. I said, "We have to open it, Kenny, someone is hurt."

Momma had heard the scream and came running as fast as she could. She yelled at us, "I thought you two were down in the field! Go down to the house, NOW!" But it was too late, I had pulled the door open and there was a woman curled up in the corner, crying with wild hair and scary eyes. I did not know what to do. Momma pushed us aside, went over to her and took her in her arms and said, "Boys, this is Aunt Lil. She is here because she had nowhere else to go. She has been in the State Mental Hospital in Little Rock. She escaped last night and caught a ride to Aunt Ola's house, but Uncle Judd would not let her stay there. They brought her here this morning. Thank goodness Daddy had already gone to town when Judd and Ola arrived with her. Daddy would not want her here either."

Then she said, "Judd called the state hospital and they are sending hospital staff here to get her. They are on their way now."

This was unreal to Kenny and me. Kenny's eyes were bulging. We really did not know anything about an *Aunt Lil* and now we were told this screaming woman with wild hair and scary eyes was our Aunt!

We looked down Shady Grove Road and saw dust flying from a big white ambulance with two men and two women in it. It had a Red Cross on the doors and the words "State Hospital." They got out with doctor's bags and a white robe of some sort. They asked us to please get out of the way. Momma started begging them to be kind to her, because she would not hurt anybody. One of the hospital women assured Momma that they would not hurt Aunt Lil. They tied her hands and feet to the ambulance stretcher and gave her a shot. In a few minutes, she stopped screaming and settled down.

Just as they were loading her into the ambulance, Daddy came running up and demanded to know what was going on. I could see Momma was dreading Daddy's return from town. He did not know about Aunt Lil escaping the hospital. Momma had only learned about it when Aunt Ola and Uncle Judd brought her to our house this morning.

Momma went over to the ambulance to try to tell Aunt Lil that she loved her, but the shot they gave Aunt Lil had already put her to sleep. Kenny and I tried to slip around to the other side to see inside the car, and to get another peek at Aunt Lil.

We watched as the big white car pulled away from our house. Neighbors were gathering around. I think they thought one of us had gone mad when they saw the State Hospital car. Aunt Ola and Uncle Judd were not in sight. I asked Momma where they were. She said nothing.

When the ambulance had gone, Daddy wanted to know how all of this had taken place. He blew his stack when he found that Ola and Judd had "dumped her" at our house. Everything was moving too fast. Kenny and I could hardly breathe. Kenny wanted to know, "Who is this *Aunt Lil*, and does this mean that Clyde and I are also going to have to go to the mental hospital someday since she is related to us?" I did not know the answer myself, but I told Kenny that Lil was his great aunt and so he probably did not have to worry. He said, "OK but what about you? She is your AUNT!" I said, "But she is Momma's half sister and I am pretty sure that Momma's half is safe. I did not have a clue what I was talking about, but Kenny felt better.

That afternoon we all sat in the shade in the metal lawn chairs and tried to sort everything out. Momma felt terrible that Kenny and I had discovered Aunt Lil in "our clubhouse." Daddy was still fuming about Aunt Ola and Uncle Judd not doing their part by keeping her at their house until the hospital arrived and for exposing Kenny and I to all this mess. My sisters, Sue and Mary, arrived. They were both crying. They had been in town and heard from neighbors, as they walked home, that someone at our house had gone nuts and the State Hospital had to come to take someone away.

We finally got everyone settled down. Momma made some sweet tea. Aunt Ola and Uncle Judd came by and tried to apologize. We all sat and fanned ourselves with the cardboard fans. Sue and Mary kept crying off and on, saying, "What will the neighbors think?"

I told Kenny that we should go back to Gerard's pond for another swim. I hoped he would not have nightmares over this. He had only turned eight years old three months ago. This had been a lot for an eight-year-old. Thank goodness I was eleven, but I wasn't sure I was ready for this experience either.

Aunt Lil died a short time later in the hospital. Momma, Daddy, Uncle Judd and Aunt Ola went to claim her body for burial. Her two brothers, Uncle Marvin and Uncle Eli and her other sister, Aunt Hilda, (all from Tennessee) came for the burial. No one else attended.

After that we always called the shed, *Aunt Lil's Shed*. We never went into it again.

Uncle Judd cuts off His Fingers

One day Uncle Judd and Aunt Ola came by our house. They had just returned from the hospital in Little Rock. Uncle Judd's right hand was bandaged. It looked very serious. Momma and I wanted to know what happened. He told us that he was running a large log through his sawmill and the log jammed. He went over to give it a push, but slipped and fell. His hand went into the saw and he cut off his thumb and index finger, so he only had three fingers left on his right hand.

We asked who drove him to the hospital in Little Rock, which was a half hour away. He said, "Well, Skinny (his nickname for Aunt Ola, although she was far from skinny) does not know how to drive, and there was no one else, so I drove myself." He said that Aunt Ola had bandaged it from of an old sheet that she tore into strips. She went with him to try to make sure he did not pass-out as they drove to the hospital. He laughed, saying, "I don't know what Skinny would have done if I had passed out because she does not have a clue about what to do to stop the truck. I guess I should try to teach her to drive." Aunt Ola replied, "No, I do not need to learn to drive, you just need to be more careful around the saws. A woman's place is in the home, not driving cars or trucks!"

Daddy had come into the house and overheard all of this. He said nothing at first, but had a smirk on his face. He had told me before that Uncle Judd was a bit careless around equipment. There was no love lost on Daddy's part toward Uncle Judd. Daddy called him "dough belly" when he was speaking to me about him. I was not sure if Daddy called him that because he had a lot of money or "dough" or if he called him that because Uncle Judd was a bit fat around his middle and the term referred to that. Uncle Judd had hired Daddy from time to time to work in his sawmill. Daddy felt that Uncle Judd had not paid him for all the hours when he last worked for him. This created a problem between Momma and Aunt Ola since they were half sisters and also "sisters" in the church. They had agreed to let the men work it out and not let it affect their relationship.

Uncle Judd looked at Daddy and said, "Mac, I need your help at the mill. It is going to be a while until my hand heals enough for me to go back to work." Daddy gave Uncle Judd a long look and said nothing. Momma and Aunt Ola looked nervous. I stood there and kept my mouth shut. I, too, was a bit nervous. Daddy and Uncle Judd just stood there staring at each other.

I saw Momma's eyes shut and her lips moving. I think she was praying. All of a sudden Momma said, "Why don't we all sit down and have a glass of sweet iced tea, since it is so hot today." Aunt Ola chimed in, "Louise, do you have any of that pineapple upside-down cake that you make so beautifully?" Momma said, "Yes, I sure do," and headed for the kitchen.

We all knew what was taking place, but we also knew that something had to be done to break the tension. Momma made the iced tea, cut the cake and we all sat down. Daddy and Uncle Judd still had said nothing to each other.

We started eating and Aunt Ola said, "Mac, you lost your index finger on your right hand a number of years ago. Remind me how that happened." Daddy did not want to take her bait, but finally said, "I got it smashed off while I was working on an Otis Elevator. An idiot I was working with started the elevator without asking me if I was in the clear and the door slammed shut on my finger." Uncle Judd said, "I bet that hurt like hell, Mac." Daddy answered, "Yes, they say that a smashed finger hurts a lot more than a finger being cut off." Uncle

Judd did not say anything back. He knew that Daddy had him "where he wanted him."

The tea was gone, and we all sat around fanning ourselves with the cardboard fans from the Ashby Funeral Home. Finally Daddy said, "Judd, you are in a fix. I will help you for a while, but I set the rules." Uncle Judd said, "Thanks, Mac. I appreciate this. Can you start working tomorrow?" Daddy said, "The minimum wage in Arkansas is seventy-five cents an hour, but since I will be the foreman, I want you to pay me ninety-five cents an hour." Judd said, "You will only be overseeing one other worker, so I will pay you eighty-five cents an hour." Daddy said, "Take your three fingers and get out of here!" Judd backed down and said OK to the ninety-five cents. Then Daddy had one more thing to say. He told Judd that he was going to write down the hours he worked each day and have Judd sign the piece of paper before Daddy left for home. Judd agreed.

After Aunt Ola and Uncle Judd went home, Momma told Daddy that she was happy that he was going to help Uncle Judd. She said, "We can use the money, and remember that we depend on Judd carrying us to town and to church in his car." This reminder only made Daddy mad again. He just replied, "That is why I did not ask for a dollar an hour."

We survived the uncomfortable situation and Daddy worked at the mill until Judd's hand healed enough for him to take over again. Daddy was sure not to let "dough-belly" cheat him. Momma, Kenny and me continued to ride to town and church in Uncle Judd's car. Daddy never did ride. He preferred to walk.

The Two-Hole Toilet

When Daddy bought the little house on Shady Grove Road there were two outdoor toilets on the property. The house had been a dance hall so it had two outhouses, one for men and one for women.

He tore one of them down and rebuilt the other one. He made it more usable by adding an extra hole, a smaller one for kids and a larger one for adults. This worked great for Kenny and me. We spent hours sitting in the outhouse and reading a catalog. There were always two catalogs in the outhouse, a Sears and Roebucks and a Montgomery Ward. The family liked Sears better, so everyone knew to use the Montgomery Ward for wiping and save the Sears catalog to read while sitting there. We did not use corncobs like our neighbors, the Johnsons. We considered people who used corncobs as hillbillies, real poor country people, and ones that did not know better or did not have money for a stamp to send for a free catalog.

Daddy threw lime into the toilet to help with the smell, especially during the hot sweaty summers. The smell was bad but it did not keep Kenny and me from sitting and looking at the Sears bicycles. We dreamed of someday owning a new bike.

We would sometimes sit there side by side and talk about things that had happened to us. One day while sitting and talking, I asked Kenny if he remembered when he was about four years old and we were playing in the yard and he bit me on the arm. He said he did not remember it, since that was five years ago. I told him I would tell him the story:

We had been playing in the backyard for a while, then for some reason you became mad at me and bit me really hard. It left your teeth marks on my arm. You had never done anything like that before. Your Momma (who was my older sister, Lucy) was there and saw it happen. She immediately grabbed you, held you and told me that I had to bite you back so you would know how it felt and you would not bite any more. My Momma was there too and grabbed me and squeezed my arm and said, "No Clyde, you are not to bite him back." Your Momma was saying for me to bite you and my Momma was saying not too. I did not know what to do, so I just grabbed your arm and bit it. I will always remember the horrible feeling I got when my teeth bit through your skin into your living flesh. It was awful. I left my teeth marks on your arm.

Momma grabbed me by the arm and hauled me down to the outhouse, pushed me inside and locked the door from the outside (Daddy had put a latch on the outside to lock when storms came up so the door would not tear off its hinges). She said for me to stay there until she let me out. I had to be punished for disobeying her. Your Momma started begging my Momma to let me out. You were crying both from my biting you and from me being locked in the outhouse. My Momma told you and your Momma to go back up to the house with her. You did.

I sat there alone and started to cry. I felt terrible, not from being locked up, but because I had bitten you, and I was sorry that I had disobeyed Momma. In a few minutes I heard you whimpering outside the outhouse. Even though you were only about four years old, you had slipped back down and tried to jump up and unlock the latch, but you were not tall enough. You looked through the crack in the door and said you were sorry. I asked you to go back to the house so you would not get in more trouble. You left.

In about an hour, I heard Daddy and Momma talking up near the house. Daddy had just come home and she was telling him what had happened. In a few minutes I heard him come to the outhouse and unlock the door. He looked at me and said, "Did you get all the catalog read?" That was all he said. I think that he thought that Momma had over-reacted, but he never said so.

I ran and found you and we hugged each other and were friends and brothers again.

After that, you never bit into any flesh except beef. You had learned your lesson, and so had I.

The Burning Tree

It was almost Christmas. My older brother, Willy, came by our house and asked Kenny and me if we wanted to go with him into the woods to find a Christmas tree. We said "sure" and went and got Daddy's handsaw.

Willy said he was going to take his twenty-two rifle in case we saw a squirrel. He liked to eat them. He said we were going into the woods down by Mr. Gerard's pond.

We were walking along and Willy told us, "Be quiet and watch for squirrels." So we did. We walked and walked and walked and suddenly Willy fired a shot from his gun. The squirrel went tearing through the trees and then ran down into the top of a dead tree. It was about twenty feet tall. Willy said, "He probably has a nest in the old hollow tree. We will smoke him out."

We gathered some dry leaves and built a tiny fire in the base of the tree, just enough to make a little smoke. All of a sudden the squirrel shot out of the top of the tree and Willy started running through the woods trying to shoot it on the run. We ran after him and the squirrel. We finally lost track of the squirrel.

Willy said, "We had better look for what we came after". We walked for another twenty minutes and finally spotted a nice Christmas tree for our house.

We cut it down and headed back towards the house, the way we had come, again near Mr. Gerard's pond. We were winding our way through the woods when we heard a strange sound. Willy stopped. "What is that sound?" We all listened. Willy looked frightened.

"Oh, my God," he said. "The sound is the old hollow tree burning." It was making a roaring sound. It was unbelievably loud. We ran near it and the whole tree was ablaze, fire shooting out the top. It had its own built-in chimney.

Willy was startled. We had forgotten all about leaving a small fire in the tree when we took off after the dumb squirrel. Now we had a big mess on our hands. I asked, "What are we going to do?" Willy said, " We can't let the tree catch the rest of the woods on fire. Mr. Gerard has his prize Hereford cows in the nearby field and it may catch on fire too."

"We will just have to wait until the tree burns enough to fall," Willy said. Kenny was not saying a thing, but his eyes were as big as cow pies. Willy told us to gather up old buckets and cans that someone had dumped here years before. We filled them from the creek that flowed from the pond. We had about ten of them filled and sat them as near the tree as we dared. Of course we had no idea which way the tree would fall once it burned enough.

We waited and waited. Finally the tree started to tremble. All of a sudden it came crashing to the ground. It was a scary sight to see. Willy yelled to us, "Start pouring cans and buckets of water on it, then run to the creek and get more water." We ran and we filled buckets and we poured water over and over again until we finally got the fire out. We were all pooped.

We picked up our Christmas tree and headed for the house. When we got there Daddy said, "Boys, you were gone a long time just to cut a Christmas tree. There must have been something else interesting in the woods for you to take so long."

There was, but we waited several days before we told Daddy what was in the woods that was so interesting that it lasted all afternoon.

One thing that I learned from this experience was that a squirrel for dinner was just not worth it. I really didn't care for squirrel meat, anyway.

The Circus Comes to Town

My brother Willy and his family lived in Bryant. It was about six miles from my house.

Willy and his wife, Tebby, stopped by one spring afternoon and asked Kenny and me if we would like to go with them to the circus. Kenny and I had ridden our bikes into town that morning to watch the circus parade. We were delighted that we were going to get to go.

When we arrived, everything was exciting. We had to go through the entrance gate. The carnivals and circus always had a barbed wire fence around the grounds so everyone had to pay just to get into the grounds.

We looked around the Midway for a while and then it was time for the Big Three Ring Circus to start. We chose a seat in the center section of the huge tent, about half way up the bleachers. We had great views of the whole circus.

They had a lot of different acts. We were most interested in the Flying Trapeze Artists Show and the Lion Trainer Show. We loved seeing the people flying through the air. It scared us too, because we were sure we were going to see one of them fall to their death. None did.

It was time for the lions and tigers to come into the tent for their show. Their act was in the middle ring. The cage was a bit different than I had seen in books. It was not made of metal bars. It was of heavy rope, woven like a fish net. It was attached to the ground and held up at the top by ropes tied to the top of the tent.

There was a Hindu man training the animals. He had a turban on his head. He seemed to be doing a great job. He cracked his whip and the lions and tigers would jump up on the chairs and tables and through hoops. He put his head in the opened mouth of one of the lions. That really scared me. I was sure we were going to see a headless body rolling on the ground. But it did not bite.

Suddenly, a huge wind started howling. Arkansas was known to have a lot of tornados and storms in the springtime. The lights blinked, the tent started to rise, the tent shuddered, then all the lights went out. Total darkness. The wind picked up the entire tent. It came crashing down on all the people. People were screaming. Men were taking out their pocketknives and slitting the heavy canvas tent in order to get out from under the weight.

When the tent fell, the lion's cage fell too. Everyone realized this. Everyone was screaming. Kenny started praying, "Lord, don't let us be eaten by a lion!" I said, "Kenny we have to get out of here. Now! Pray later."

We found our way in the dark up to the top bleachers. There we were able to jump down about eight feet to the ground, again in the dark. We were too scared to stop to see if we were all right. We saw a circus truck parked right outside the tent. We ran and crawled under the truck. Others were trying to get under the truck, too. The wind was blowing dust to the point of us not being able to see very much.

We did not know if the lions were going to kill us, or whether the tornado would do the job. Kenny was praying again. I encouraged him to continue this time. All of a sudden, my brother and his wife somehow found us under the truck. I felt better with Willy being there. Of course, the lions could eat him too. He had blood running down his face. He said one of the smaller tent poles struck him when the tent fell.

Willy said, "We have got to get to our car before one of those lions gets somebody." We all started to run in the direction of the car. Everybody else was trying to do the same. In our panic, we all forgot about the barbed wire fence. We were all running into it and tearing our clothes and skin. Finally the fence went down under the crush. People started tripping over it and falling on top of each other.

We made it to the car and only felt safe when we got the doors shut. Kenny's prayer had worked. We hurried home as fast as we could. We had enough of the circus.

The next morning the local radio newsman reported about the circus fiasco. He said there was only one person that was critically hurt. It was a young girl named Judy. MY COUSIN! We had not heard about her being hurt. She had been sitting on the opposite side of the tent. We did not know that she was there, too. She was caught between the rows of bleachers as they crashed to the ground. Her pelvis was broken.

The radio said she was crushed when the bleachers collapsed as everyone jumped up. They said many people were hurt from the weight of the tent falling on them, none seriously.

The announcer went on to say, "No one was hurt by the lions. The circus people were able to lift the tent high enough to back a circus truck under the tent. The Hindu trainer took each lion by the neck and led it into the truck. The lions stayed pretty calm, according to the trainer."

By daybreak, the circus had packed up the entire circus and left town. They had overheard town men talking about the circus workers not having put the tent stakes in the ground deep enough. Their three-day show did not make it through the first twenty-four hours. It was best that they left town when they did.

I did not plan to go inside any big tent again, and that included a preacher's revival tent. They just were not a safe place for a young boy. Kenny said he agreed with my thoughts on this. Kenny was one smart boy.

Beautiful Bugs

Kenny and I were afraid of snakes. All kinds. But we liked bugs, except the biting kind. We hated ticks and chiggers.

In the spring there were always beautiful iridescent green beetle-like bugs that arrived in June. We called them June bugs because of the month of their arrival. Someone told us that they were Japanese

Beetles. We did not tell Daddy that someone told us this name, as he did not like anything with the name Japan in it. He was having a hard time forgetting the war, I thought.

We each caught a large beetle and tied a piece of sewing thread about three feet long to one of its legs. We made a bow-tie knot so we could untie it later.

We let the bugs fly to the end of their string. Sometimes we played all day with them, even put them in our pockets for safe keeping when we made ourselves a peanut and Karo corn syrup sandwich for lunch. We were always very careful when taking them out of our pockets so we didn't hurt them.

At the end of the day we would untie the string and let them go back to their families.

Nighttime was a special time for people who lived out in the country. My family always sat outside on metal lawn chairs and swatted mosquitos and looked at the millions of stars and watched the lightning bugs. They made a beautiful mosaic out of the darkness surrounding our house.

Country people have better darkness than city people. It was a real deep dark and the night creatures would put on a magnificent light show free for us every night.

Sometimes we caught a lot of lightning bugs and put them in a quart Mason jar. We attached a wire handle and carried it like a lantern. It was fun to take our lantern and make our way to the outhouse and sit. Kenny would sit on the small hole, and me on the larger one. We would try to see if we could read the catalog with the glow from our lanterns.

Momma always made us open the jar and let the lightning bugs out before we went to bed, so they could light up the skies again tomorrow night. We wanted to take them to bed with us but she would not hear of it.

She was a good Momma.

Daddy's Pistol

One day I asked my Daddy if he would tell me some stories of the old days when he was a young man. My Daddy was born in 1881.

President Lincoln was assassinated only sixteen years before my Daddy was born.

Daddy was born in a small town in rural western Tennessee. He lived with several brothers and his parents. I never got to meet my Daddy's parents or my Mother's parents as they all had died before I was born.

Daddy told me he was going to tell me two stories about how he had to use his pistol to get out of a couple of jams, as he called it.

He said that when he was about thirty-five years old, he took a trip over into Arkansas to see about some Delta land. He had heard that land was for sale. He thought he might have an interest in it.

This was 1916 and there were only dirt mud roads in the south. He started to Arkansas in the evening after work. He had saved his money and had purchased a new Model T Ford coupe. He said he was very proud of it.

He crossed the mighty Mississippi River on a large raft car ferry. There were three other cars on the ferry. One of the cars had several men in it. They were rather loud and not very nice. They made a few remarks about my Daddy's shiny new Ford coupe and talked about how much it must have cost him.

He said he did not respond to them because he thought they were up to no good. Their car was the first one off the ferry and Daddy's car was the last to leave the boat. It was now getting dusk and he had at least another hour and a half to drive before getting to Jonesboro where the Delta land was listed for sale.

He stopped at a little roadside store, went in and had a cup of coffee, then got back in the Ford and headed towards Jonesboro.

It had been raining for the past few days and the dirt and black delta soil combined made for a muddy road. He said that his Ford was making its way along without getting stuck or even spinning his wheels. He was very pleased with the way things were going.

He came over a little hill and he saw the taillights of a car stopped ahead. It appeared to be stuck in the mud. As he got closer he could see that it was the same men who were saying nasty things about his car on the ferry.

The thought hit Daddy that they were only acting like their car was stuck. He thought that when he pulled up behind them to try to help, they might jump him and rob him. He stopped his car about 100 feet before their car and got out of his Ford.

They shouted, "Come and help us push our car out of the mud." He did not answer. Instead he took his Smith and Wesson pistol out from under the seat of his car. He fired two shots into the air. He yelled, "Get that God Damned car out of the mud and leave. I still have four more bullets left, one for each of you."

He said they crawled all over each other trying to get into their car. They started the engine and tore out of the mud and out of sight with mud slinging out from their tires.

Daddy said, "It was amazing how unstuck they got when they had a gun stuck in their faces."

In those days there were not many sheriffs around and each man had to protect himself.

The other story he told me also happened at night while traveling in rural Tennessee. He was staying overnight at a rooming house in the small town of Huntington. He had met a girl in the rooming house cafe. They started a conversation. He thought she was pretty. He was not yet married to my Momma; they would not get married for a long time.

The pretty girl was flirting with him and said, "Why don't you drop by my house after dark and we can talk some more. Be sure that it is dark because Daddy goes to bed shortly after dark. Don't drive your car because Daddy will hear it. Just walk up the road and my house will be the first house on the right side of the road. It is only a short walk." Daddy said he was pretty excited. She sure was pretty.

He had supper at the rooming house, washed his face and waited until dark. Just before he left his room, he thought of his pistol and went and got it from under the front seat of his car. He had a funny feeling come over him, a feeling of mistrust.

He walked beyond the edge of the small town and headed up the dirt road as the pretty girl had told him to do. She said it was not very far to her house. He started walking. It was a very dark night, no moon in sight, just millions of stars. He started looking for the oil lamp's glow from her house. He saw none and thought he needed to walk a little farther. Then he stopped dead in his tracks.

Ahead, off the left side of the dirt road he saw the glow of a cigarette and then the glow was gone. A chill went through him. Someone in the bushes was waiting to ambush Daddy.

He pulled out his pistol and aimed it a few feet above where he had seen the glowing cigarette and fired two shots. He heard bushes breaking as, whoever it was, went scrambling out of the bushes and running away.

Daddy yelled, "Come back, you coward. I will show you how many bullets I have left." The guy did not come back.

Daddy turned back to town and got into his car. He wanted to see if there really was a house, just up the road on the right. He drove about three miles before he finally spotted a house on the right side of the road. All the lights were out. It looked abandoned. Daddy felt real bad about being made a fool of by such a pretty young woman.

After that, he always wondered if the pretty girl was working with the owner of the rooming house to lure young men staying there into a trap.

The next morning Daddy asked the man who ran the rooming house if he knew who the girl was that he was talking to yesterday at the table. The man said he had never seen her before. Daddy doubted it.

In Spring We Burn the Lawn

Every spring, Daddy thought we should burn off the old dead Bermuda grass in our yard before the new grass started to grow. We had an old push lawnmower, and Daddy said by burning off the old grass, the new grass would be easier to mow.

Before we started the burn, we had to prepare so we would not allow the fire to get out of control or too near our wooden house. There was no foundation around our house. It sat upon posts with the front of the house right down on the ground and the back of the house was off the ground about two feet, due to the sloping yard.

Daddy had Kenny and I go to the well and get two buckets of water each. We poured them into a galvanized washtub. He took old toe sacks (burlap) and pine boughs and soaked them in the water. These would be used to beat back the fire from where we did not want it to go, like under the house.

We always tried to make sure there was no wind blowing, because that could really get the fire going too fast.

It was time to start the burn. Daddy said, "Ready, boys? We have to keep a close eye on the fire." He started the burn near the house. A very slight wind was blowing away from the house, so this would take the fire away from the house. Perfect. This was what we wanted to happen. All of a sudden, the wind switched and started to blow a bit harder towards the house.

Daddy started yelling, "Start fighting the fire! Keep dipping in the water and hitting the fire!" The fire was coming towards us. It was trapping us between the flames and the house. We were hitting the fire for all we were worth. Momma heard Daddy yelling. She came and started helping us beat the fire. Some of the fire was getting near the side of the house.

All of a sudden, the wind switched again away from the house. It started to move back out into the yard. We had saved the house. Daddy had tears in his eyes. He knew we had almost lost the house and possibly burned us too. He had fear in his eyes along with tears. Momma was a nervous wreck. Kenny and I were trying to wipe the smoke out of our eyes.

I said to Kenny, "Were you praying for the wind to change?" "Yeah," he said. "I didn't know what else to do." Daddy came over and gave Kenny a big hug. He said, "You done good, Kenny." Kenny had a big smile on his face, a sooty face with white teeth showing as it broke into a big grin.

Poor, But Happy

When one is raised in a poor family, it does not take a lot to make one happy. Happiness does not come just from obtaining monetary things, but by experiencing happiness in the family environs.

I still cherish the thoughts of my Mother making biscuits with white gravy, fried okra, and homemade pies and cakes.

I have beautiful remembrances of the family sitting around the radio in the winter evenings listening to our favorite shows, as well as sitting outside on metal lawn chairs in the deep dark of the summer night watching the glorious display put on for us by the lightning bugs while we simply talked.

I cherish the memory of my Mother saving her money to buy an easel for me because she knew I wanted to be an artist someday. These are the kind of things that can make a poor boy happy. I was.

Christmas, a Special Event

It was Christmas, 1948. I was seven years old.

Christmas was so magical to me. Daddy and I always went into the woods to find a cedar tree to cut and put up in our living room.

We decorated it with some older glass ornaments that Aunt Madeline gave to us when she bought herself some new ones. I thought they were beautiful, old or not. She gave us some beautiful tinsel roping, too, to wrap around the tree. We also made strings of popcorn to put around the tree. I made a star out of cardboard and covered it with tinfoil and placed it on top of the tree. We did not have colored electric bulbs on our tree like some of our neighbors did. Daddy said we could not afford them. I understood.

On Christmas Eve Momma told me, "Santa will bring some gifts and leave them under the tree tonight." I wanted to believe in Santa, but we didn't have a chimney. Momma said, "He has a key to our front door." That was good enough for me.

When I went to bed, I could not go to sleep. I lay awake and listened for the key in the front door. I fell asleep before the key rattled in the door.

Christmas morning I awoke early and headed into the living room. Momma and Daddy followed me in. There were some presents under the tree wrapped in pretty Christmas paper. I could not believe that Santa would do all this for us. There were three presents with my name on them and one with Kenny's on it. Kenny was my oldest sister's son. He was three years younger than me, but we considered ourselves "brothers." He and his Momma lived just down the road from us. Kenny's Daddy had died from tuberculosis.

I didn't understand why Santa did not know that Kenny does not live here. Momma explained, "Santa left it here for Kenny so he will have a present to open when he comes up to our house later this morning."

In addition to my three presents there was also a basket under the tree with oranges, apples and nuts; all kinds of nuts and ribbon candy too. I was so happy.

I asked if I could open my presents. I opened one. It was a metal wind-up car. I wound it up and put it on the table. It ran to the edge of the table, but did not fall off. It always turned and stayed on the table.

I opened another one. It was a Hopalong Cassidy cowboy pistol and real leather holster, with rolls of caps that popped when you pulled the trigger. My third present was a cowboy shirt with beautiful designs sewn into it.

After I opened the presents, Momma told me to save the wrapping paper so that it could be used again next year. So, I carefully smoothed it out and gave it to her. The question came to my mind, "How does Santa get the wrapping paper back from Momma so he will have it to wrap presents for me again next Christmas?" Part of the magic, I guessed.

This was a wonderful Christmas. How could Santa know what each kid would like for Christmas?

Momma fixed breakfast and said, "Kenny and his Momma will be up to our house in a little while." I could not wait to show him what I got.

When Kenny arrived, he had a bag filled with his new toys. He said, "Hey Clyde, Santa left a present for you at our house." I was not sure what to think about Santa. He was a bit confused, I thought.

Kenny unpacked his bag. He too had a cowboy gun and leather holster set, just like mine. He also had a new cowboy shirt that was a different color than mine. He had a wind-up car that was also a different color. We both laughed.

We each opened the other two gifts that Santa left for us. Kenny had a beautiful red metal convertible car and I had the same one, only it was beautiful yellow color.

After we played for a while with our new toys we asked our parents, "What did Santa bring you?" They told us, "Santa only brings presents for kids."

It had snowed during the night. Kenny and I took a big pan and went out and scooped new snow into it. We brought it into the kitchen, put a few drops of vanilla, some sugar, some milk and stirred it. Then we put it into three bowls and poured a few drops of red and green food coloring on it. We called Momma, Daddy and Kenny's Momma into the kitchen.

We presented them with our homemade snow Christmas Ice Cream that we made just for them. They smiled and ate it even though it was only ten o'clock on Christmas morning.

We wished them Merry Christmas and told them this was the best Christmas we could ever have.

My First Bicycle

Daddy said, "Now that you are six years old, perhaps Santa will bring you a bike for Christmas." I was very excited. I had been learning to ride Charlie Smith's bike, so I was ready for my own.

On Christmas morning I awoke early and went into the living room to see if Santa had brought a bike for me.

When I saw the Christmas tree, there was a green Columbia bike standing there with a red bow on it. But, there was a problem. It was a girl's bike, and it was a used bike. I did not know that Santa brought used toys to kids.

It looked fine and was my favorite color, but it was a girl's bike! Girl's bikes don't have a bar so a girl can wear a skirt and peddle a bike. Did Santa think I was a girl? Is he getting too old to be doing his job?

Boys needed boy's bikes with a bar from the seat to the handle bar area. I didn't wear a skirt. I wore pants. I needed a bar.

Momma and Daddy saw my disappointment. Daddy said," Santa must have gotten mixed up, but, don't worry. We will have a bar welded across the bike tomorrow at the welder's shop."

So the next day we put the bike in the back of Uncle Judd's truck and took it to the welder. He welded a bar on it and we brought it home.

I repainted the entire bike a new green color and it looked great. I don't think Santa would recognize it now.

Now I had a pretty green boy's bike. I still could not understand Santa getting me mixed up for a girl. I have never worn a skirt in my life.

The Price of Coffee

Daddy was cursing as he came down the road. He had just walked three miles from town. He was fuming, angry and saying a few new words that I did not know.

He told us, "When I ordered a cup of coffee in the Triangle Cafe, they told me that coffee had gone up from five cents to ten cents a cup!" "That is double the price!" he shouted. "This is highway robbery! This cannot be tolerated. This sounds like something the Republicans have done."

On the way home, he wanted to see if the price of a pound of coffee had increased as well. He stopped at the grocery store to check the price. The price of a pound of coffee had gone from thirty-five cents to fifty-nine cents!

He continued his rage, "If Mr. Roosevelt were still alive, he would not have allowed this to happen. The next thing you will see is bread costing twenty-five cents a loaf and gasoline will be a quarter a gallon. Postage stamps will go from three cents per stamp to four cents. There will be no end to this thing they are calling inflation."

"The poor people and us, who are a little short on money, are going to hurt in a bad way," he said. Then he told Momma and me that we had to start being more careful using electricity in our house. He said to be sure and turn off the light when you leave each room. He said our electric bill last month was two dollars and that was just getting too high.

The next day Daddy said he was going to protest the new price of coffee. He was going to start drinking hot water with sugar in it, instead of coffee.

I liked to drink coffee with Daddy and the idea of hot water and sugar did not sound good to me. I told Daddy, "I will pick up cold drink bottles each month to help pay for the new double price of coffee." He wanted to protest the high price, but he liked his coffee, too.

I thought with my help, and if they don't double the price again, we should be saved from drinking hot water with sugar.

Cowboy Boots

We found the greatest treasures that people threw away along the sides of country roads. We found old bike wheels and wagon wheels that we could use to make our own carts. One day we found a pair of kid's cowboy boots that someone had thrown away. They still had a lot of use in them. Kenny discovered them first. He tried them on and they were a bit big for his feet. I tried them on and they were a bit tight on mine.

I said to Kenny, "Shoes that are too loose on your feet can cause serious foot problems." I continued, "Even though they are a bit tight on my feet, they will stretch, so I should have them." He did not like the idea but did not want to have serious foot problems.

I pulled and pulled to get them on. They were tight but I was going to wear them. We rode our bikes into town to Mr. Gingle's shoe store where he had a Fluoroscope x-ray machine. You stood and put your feet into it to see how your new shoes fit your feet. We would stop by his store at least once a week just to look at our feet. The screen that you looked in was a beautiful green color.

I stuck my feet into the machine and looked down through the screen. All I could see were bones of my very cramped feet in tiny boots. The store man came over to look. He looked at the screen, then at me. He told me, "If you wear those boots, your toes are going to curl under your feet."

I took the boots off and asked the man for some tissue paper. We wadded it up. I had Kenny put on the boots. Then I stuffed it down in the boots, behind Kenny's heels, so they fit him better.

Kenny did look sharp in those boots. I told him that within a year he would grow right into them. I never did have a pair of cowboy boots, but I had a sidekick that did.

Biscuits, our Daily Bread

Every day of the year, except Christmas morning, my Momma would make biscuits for our breakfast. She would fry an egg and we always had white flour gravy to pour over the biscuits. We would cut some of the biscuits in half, put in a gob of butter, and then add the homemade jam that she made from berries or wild plums. She would fry some bacon for my Daddy and me. She did not eat bacon because she said, "The Bible says you should not eat pigs." Daddy let me drink coffee with him, but said, "You have to drink it black like a real man does." Sugar and milk sure would have tasted better in it, but only if you were a girl or a weenie of a guy.

Once a week Momma would make me a fried pie for breakfast with apples and cinnamon in it. She would roll out a piece of dough, lay a saucer up-side down on the dough, take a paring knife and cut around the edge of the saucer to make a circle. She put in fruit, sugar and some butter, then folded the dough in half and pinched the edges together into a half moon. She dropped it in the hot oil of the iron skillet.

Man, did I love those pies. The only thing better was once in a while she would put sugar and butter and cinnamon instead of apples and pinch around the edges and fry that. Now that, with black coffee, was a real man's breakfast.

On Christmas morning, my Momma did not make biscuits. I think she thought Santa should make them. He never did.

Congo Grocery and Mercantile

Eight miles up Congo Road was the Congo Mercantile Store. It was way out in the country. They had groceries, cow and horse feed, barbed wire, tools, tires, car parts, work clothes and candy.

They had a big orange truck with a canvas covering over the back, just like the trucks that we would see on the highway hauling Mexicans some place to pick fruit or something.

The Congo truck was used to deliver groceries and cow feed to people who did not have a car or truck. We did not have either. All you had to do was send a list of groceries in the mail and they'd be delivered in a day or two.

My Momma had worked out a plan with our postman with the ugly Nash car, to meet him at our mailbox and give him her grocery list on his way up Congo Road. Then he would drop off the list at the Congo Mercantile. That way we could get our groceries delivered the same day we ordered them. He would take her envelope with the stamp attached and with his fountain pen make an X on the postage stamp. He said, "There is no need to take it back to town to get the stamp cancelled."

Later that same day, the big orange truck with the canvas would drive up to the front of our house and honk his horn. We would all go out front to get our groceries and cow feed. The driver always had some penny candy for Kenny and me. We liked him a lot.

We always got a kick out of seeing what Momma ordered. She would order Duz washing powder soap because the box would always have a drinking glass or a cereal bowl mixed in with the soap powder. The box said *Duz Duz Everything*.

Momma also bought Welch's Grape Jelly in pretty designed drinking glasses. She was trying to get a dozen of them. But what I liked best was she would buy a small glass of Kraft Pimiento Cream Cheese or Pineapple Creamed Cheese. We had to eat it very slowly as it was expensive. I think she tried to splurge a little now and then.

The cow feed sacks were made of printed cotton material. Momma would make herself a pretty dress out of the sacks on her treadle Singer Sewing Machine. You had to cut the string at the top of the sack and open carefully so as not to damage the pretty printed cloth.

At the church potluck dinner, you could tell which woman had bought the same brand of cow feed that we did.

My Momma's New Linoleum

Spring had arrived and Momma was trying to get things fixed up a bit. To me, this meant that Aunt Madeline would be coming to visit again.

Momma had been saving up a few dollars so she could order a new linoleum for our living room. The old one had quite a few tears around the edges.

She sent a letter to the Congo Mercantile store and told them to pick out a pretty 9'x12' one with red roses and some sort of green background.

The day before the Congo delivery truck arrived, Daddy and I rolled up the old linoleum and carried it down to the gully in the field. We went back to the house and painted a brown two-foot border around the floor of the room near the walls. Now when we put down the new linoleum, the room would glow.

The day the truck arrived we were all waiting and excited. Momma had made a large pitcher of fresh sweet tea and some homemade cookies. She had invited Fricky and Gus Johnson, as well as a couple of other neighbors, to see her new purchase.

The linoleum was laid, the tea was poured and the cookies served. We all sat around the living room. The women talked about how beautiful the red roses were on the green background. The men said, "Yes, they are pretty," then talked about the weather.

When everyone went home Momma had a smile on her face. I could see she was so pleased. I told her, "Momma, I want to sleep on a pallet on the new linoleum tonight." She said, "That is fine with me." We got a quilt from the trunk, folded it, made a pallet and I went to sleep on my Momma's new bed of roses.

Our New Bicycles

I had an old bike that my Momma and Daddy got for me when I was six years old. But now, Kenny and I wanted a brand-new bicycle in the worst way. We had now learned that Santa was only make-believe. It was hard for each of us to learn this fact. Before, when we did not get what we had hoped for Christmas, we simply thought that Santa did not have enough room in his sleigh, or we would come up with some other imaginative reason.

But knowing was a different thing. We knew if we could not get a new bike it was for a simple reason: Money. We got Kenny's Momma and my Momma and Daddy together to discuss it. We asked if there was some way that they might possibly be able to buy us a bike. Momma said she had been thinking about it. She said that the Western Auto Store would let a person buy things on layaway. She said this means that we put some money down on the bikes, and the store keeps the bikes until you get all the payments made.

She said the new Western Flyers were about thirty dollars each. The store would let us put five dollars down on each bike, and pay five dollars per month. The bikes had to be paid for by Christmas. There was still six months until Christmas. This was perfect.

We told our parents that we would be responsible for paying two dollars each month. We would pick up cold drink bottles along the highway and sell them.

So each month, we each had to pick up a lot of bottles from the roadside. This would give us less money to spend for candy, but it would be worth it.

Every month, we turned our two dollars into our Mommas. They added three dollars to make the layaway payments.

On Christmas morning Kenny got a beautiful blue 24" Western Flyer bike and I got a red 26" one. It was snowing. This was a rare occasion in Central Arkansas. We did not care. We jumped on our new bicycles and raced up and down the road, sliding from one side to the other. We were thrilled to own brand-new bicycles!

After riding for a while, we went into the house and hugged our parents and told them, "We just love our new bikes so much! Thank you for making our Christmas so happy."

When it Rained, It Leaked

When it rained the old tin roof on our house always leaked. Tin roofs were wonderful for listening to the rain, especially at night when I snuggled under the covers. I would lie in bed and listen to the rain change tunes, sometimes it was like a drumroll when it poured buckets-full and some times like a tea kettle when it rained more softly. I loved the sounds, especially the thunder that was sometimes so loud that you would almost jump out of bed. I knew as I listened that the tin cans Daddy had placed around the attic floor were filling. Daddy and I would have to crawl up the ladder the next morning to empty them.

Momma, Daddy and I were eating breakfast when he said, "Some storm last night; I think we need to empty the tin cans in the attic this morning. One of them must have filled and run over, because I saw a water spot on the living room ceiling this morning. Guess if it is going to rain that hard, I will have to put a larger can or a pan under that leak."

After breakfast, we took a large water bucket; two coffee cans and crawled up the wooden ladder that Daddy built. In the attic, you had to be careful where you stepped because there was no floor in the attic, only the ceiling joist to step on. We went from can to can (there were about fifteen of them spread around). We emptied each one and replaced two with larger cans.

I asked Daddy why we had so many leaks in our tin roof. He said, "There really are not fifteen holes. What happens is, where there is a hole, the rain comes through, and some of it drips down right under the hole, but some of it runs down the roof rafters and drips in another place, so you need more cans to catch all the drips." Then he said, "I have crawled all over the roof trying to find the leaks. It is hard to see them from up on top of the roof. I put tar in each one I find and hope for the best."

Daddy told me that when I was younger, some repair guys came by our house. They told him they could repair the roof for fifty dollars. That was a huge amount of money for our family. Daddy trusted them and gave them the money. They painted the entire roof with a thick, aluminum stuff. It looked good, like a new roof.

They left. The next time it rained, Daddy crawled the ladder to check the cans. They were dry and he was happy. Several rains latter, he again crawled up to inspect, and found a little water in several of the cans. He came back down with a frown on his face.

Each new rain brought more leaks, more trips to the attic to empty the cans. I continued to love to listen to the sound of the rain on the tin roof. I knew it meant we would have to step carefully on the ceiling joist each time and not fall through the ceiling. It was an adventure for me, but not for Daddy.

MY EARLY SCHOOL DAYS

Schooling for me was a little unusual. My education, between first and eighth grade, was spent in both public school and church school.

Our small Seventh-day Adventist Church attempted to operate a school, which was a financial burden to the church congregation, but they felt their children should be kept away from the worldly influences that they would be exposed to in public school. My mother went along with this. She had to pay fifteen dollars a month for my tuition. She did housekeeping and was paid fifteen dollars a week, so one week of her earnings each month went to keep me in church school. My father felt that public school would be just fine for me, and they would have more money to live on.

So the church had school one year, then had to take a year off to pay the past year's debts. Then I was back to public school for a year.

I started first grade in public school. I cannot say that I learned any better or easier in one school or the other. School was pretty simple in those days.

Starting School

I was scared to start school in first grade. I had to go into town where I was not used to being and I had to ride Mr. Lacky's big yellow bus. My Momma had saved money to buy my school supplies and a satchel to carry the school things and my baloney sandwich. I was scared of school but proud of the satchel. It had a good smell. It smelled like leather with its leather handles and straps. It smelled expensive to me.

Mrs. Cabe was my first grade teacher. She was old and gray. My Daddy said she was old as dirt. She was probably my Daddy's age. The school was old, too. The room always had a smell like mop oil and color crayons. It also had old wooden bench desks where we all had to sit. My desk was right across the aisle from a pretty girl with blond hair. She was shy and would not speak to me. I think she was scared, too, like me.

When we had to go to the bathroom, Mrs. Cabe told us to hold up our hand with one finger if we had to do number one and two fingers if we had to do number two. I did not know why she had to know what we needed to do.

Every day the pretty blond girl would sit in her desk and pee her pants. Soon there was a yellow puddle under her desk. She would look at me, then down at the puddle on the floor. I was not sure what she wanted me to do. I thought maybe she needed a plug. Mrs. Cabe would come back and look disgusted and ask her why she did not hold up her hand with one finger. But this did not keep her from peeing her pants. I think my plug idea would have worked better.

After the school day was over, my next fear was being sure to get on the right bus to take me home. I would look until I saw Mr. Lacky, and then climb the steep steps. I always looked for the blond girl who peed her pants. I guess she took a different bus. It took a little while, but my fears about school and Mrs. Cabe and finding my bus eased. The pretty blond quit peeing her pants. They must have found a plug for her.

The Candy Men

One day, at public school, we had the greatest thing happen. The teachers gathered all the students into the large auditorium for a special treat. We all waited in our seats wondering what was going to happen.

The curtains on the stage opened and a little short man with a little round flat-top hat and a strange suit came out on the stage. He looked like the doorman at the big hotel in Little Rock that we walked by on the way to Woolworth's Five and Dime Store. Momma said the man at the hotel was called a bellhop.

The guy on the stage put his hands to his mouth and yelled out, "Call for Philip Morris." It was a cigarette ad that all the school kids had heard many times on the radio. There were lots of cigarette ads on the radio, but "Call for Philip Morris" was the most popular.

We all shouted back to him, "Call for Philip Morris, " and everyone clapped. He said that he hoped that our fathers smoked Philip Morris cigarettes. He had a special gift for each student. All we had to do was get in line and come up to the front of the auditorium. He would personally hand out a box of candy cigarettes with the name Philip Morris printed on them–Just like the real thing! He told us that we should only pretend we were smoking by using candy cigarettes until we were old enough to smoke Philip Morris.

Then he left the auditorium, went outside and got into his cute little sports car. We all waved and yelled goodbye to a short little man who liked us enough to bring us candy. He must have thought we were special.

A few weeks later we were again ushered into the auditorium. Another little man came out on the stage. This time he was not just short. He was a midget in a little suit and a little hat. He said he was Mr. Zero, the Zero Candy Man.

We did not know anything about Zero Candy. This brand was new for our town. Unlike Philip Morris, he did not have anything to shout out to us. He just started throwing Zero Candy bars out into the audience, to our delight. We were all trying to catch one and diving under the seats to try to get one we had missed.

He told everyone to go outside. There, he had a beautiful red sports car with Mr. Zero written on each door and across the back. He said he wanted to be sure that everyone had received a Zero Candy bar.

He told us, "Always watch for a picture of Mr. Zero near the candy shelf in your favorite store. If you want to see my picture smile, just buy a Zero Candy Bar." We thought he was teasing.

When he left, I thought, what a great job he has! He just goes around to schools and makes kids happy. If I were a midget, I would look for a job like that. But I was already taller than Mr. Zero and I was only in the fourth grade. I thought I would need to look for other work.

Shame and Lies

Being a kid from a poor family was not fun at times. I always dreaded it when the public school year started. I also dreaded the first day back to school after Christmas vacation.

The teacher would say, "Today, we are all going to tell where we traveled for summer vacation," or "We are all going tell what we got for Christmas." This was hard on a kid who had never taken a vacation or who got very few Christmas gifts.

When it came time for me to tell about my family's vacation, I would tell of going to Hot Springs for the day, or to Little Rock. Some rich kids told of going all the way to Memphis and some even went to California.

The next year I was prepared. I spent time reading about some vacation places. Then when my turn came, I would tell about going to Washington D.C. or England or to see Old Faithful at the Yellowstone National Park.

I would tell about all the wonderful things that Santa brought down the chimney for me at Christmas. The truth was we did not even have a chimney.

I would sit in my seat and wonder if the teacher understood that some of us kids were poor, or were a little short of money.

Mr. Roosevelt helped the poor people with some things, but he did not send us a Santa.

Dead Man, Single Shot to the Head

One of the most exciting things at church school was recess. We would play the game we called Dare Base. After choosing sides, half of us would line up at one side of the yard while the others lined up on the other. Then we would run out into the middle and dare someone from the other side to try to tag us before we could get back to our home base line. Of course, someone from our side could come out and try to tag the one trying to tag us.

One day during the afternoon recess we were playing Dare Base when we all heard a single gunshot ring out. At least that was what everyone thought. We all ran to where it sounded like it came from—the back of the house across the street. There was a screened porch. As we all looked in, we saw a man lying there with blood coming from his mouth and a pistol near him.

It scared all of us to death. We ran as fast as we could to tell our teacher. She was shocked and asked, "Are you sure you saw a man lying in blood?" We said, "Yes." She said she would call the police. She did, and then she told us, "You had no business going over there." She was shook up and not happy with us.

Soon we heard the sirens coming up the street. Two police cars and the Ashby's Funeral Home ambulance arrived. Police started running up to the house. Our teacher told us stay on our side of the street.

In a few minutes they brought the man out on a stretcher and put him in the ambulance and it sped away.

Then two policemen walked over to the school and asked, "Who was the one that called the police?" The teacher said she did. Then they wanted to know how we discovered the shooting. We told them that we had heard the single shot. They asked a million questions.

A little later, our teacher tried to explain to us why people commit suicide, but she did not do a very good job of it. I understood her difficulty. What could be so bad that someone would shoot himself?

This had been a recess we would never forget.

There Ain't No Such Word as Ain't

Mrs. Smithson was my sixth grade teacher in public school. She was a Yankee. They said she was from Boston. Her husband was transferred to our town for his job. The other students and I didn't think she liked us very much.

I didn't like her much, but I liked her pretty daughter, Judy. She had beautiful brown hair and very pretty brown eyes. I sat in the seat right behind her in class. Judy said it was hard for her being a student in her mother's class. She said her mother kept an eye on her too much. I agreed, because she was always watching me when I tried to talk to Judy. She was probably afraid for Judy to like a Southern boy.

One day I used the word "ain't" in class. Mrs. Smithson blew up and said to me in a very tightly controlled voice, "There is no such word as ain't. It is not in the dictionary and you are not to use it again."

I told her, "There is such a word as ain't. We use it all the time at our house. My Daddy uses it and he may not be educated, but he ain't stupid."

I thought she was going to blow a gasket. She said, "Well, you students might use it in the South, but it is not a word." I decided to shut my mouth.

Judy was embarrassed. I was embarrassed. Mrs. Smithson had shamed the whole South and me with her words.

One thing that I did know was that we Southern kids at least knew that the word car had an 'R" in it, as well as the word park, and that the word draw did not end in an "R", and neither did Florida or Africa.

Where did this woman get her fancy learning? If she was going to try to use forty-dollar words on us, she had better learn how to say them correctly–at least before she corrects us students about words that she does not even know exist.

We may have to tell her the next time that she leaves the "R" out of the word car, that there ain't no such word as "ca" in the dictionary.

I should have forgotten about Judy. I could not imagine growing up, marrying her, and having Mrs. Smithson as my *mother-in-lawr*.

My Savior in the Fire Escape Dilemma

Mrs. Carry was beautiful. She was my fourth grade teacher. She was probably about twenty-four years old. I seemed to be her favorite, but this might have been my imagination, at least that was what my Daddy told me.

One day, Mrs. Carry walked by my desk while I was drawing a picture of a cabin by a river that I remembered having seen in Aunt Ola's attic. My teacher stopped and admired it. She said she liked it a lot. She said, "Clyde, you are very talented in art."

Her remark reminded me of Aunt Ola telling me that art talent ran in our family. I said proudly, "Thank you, it runs in my family." I had never said this out loud before, and I was very pleased with how it sounded.

She then asked me if she could keep the picture. I was thrilled! "Oh, yes!" I said. I would have drawn hundreds of pictures for her if she asked. She said that I should continue doing drawings and paintings. I did, many times with Mrs. Carry in my mind.

Mrs. Carry's classroom was on the second floor of the red brick public school. The building was quite old. There was only one stairway from the first floor to the second. The Fire Department said that since the school had only one stairway, they would have to install a large fire escape so the kids on the second floor could get out of the building in case of fire.

The School Board had a large metal tube fire escape installed that went down along side the building. There was a door at the top. When you opened it, you could jump into the tube, make a sharp right turn and you would slide all the way to the bottom. There was also a door at the bottom that was kept locked at night so kids from the community would not play in it.

Mrs. Carry and the other three second floor teachers asked the principal if the children could use the new fire escape tube to slide down for recess. The principal said yes. We were delighted.

Each day when the recess bell rang, we all dashed for the opening, jumped in, and slid down to the playground with delight.

Each morning as he started his daily duties, the school janitor was to unlock the doors of the fire escape, both at the top and the bottom. At the end of the school day, he was to lock them again,.

One day, the bell rang and we all headed for the escape tube. I was the fourth kid to jump in. As we made the sharp turn at the top, we all had a horrible surprise. The door at the bottom was shut! We were all sliding into each other. We started yelling, "STOP! Don't come down! The door is locked!"

Before they heard us, more kids were jumping in and sliding into us. We were getting hurt, with everyone packing on top of us. It was terrible! Everyone started screaming!

The teachers heard the screaming and ran for the janitor. He hurriedly unlocked and opened the lower door. We all fell out. The girls were crying. The boys were trying not to cry. Some of us had gotten squashed and we were needing help. I thought my leg was broken.

The teachers ran to help us. Mrs. Carry came to where I was lying and started to examine my arms and legs. She assured me I would be all right. The pain seemed to leave me as soon as she touched me. I did not need a doctor. Mrs. Carry could perform miracles. She was all I needed.

The teachers examined all the kids that had been hurt. None seemed to be more than bruised. My leg was not broken, only sprained. There was no hospital in our town and there was only one ambulance. There were too many kids to fit into one ambulance to take us to Little Rock to the hospital to be examined.

So, the principal called two local doctors to come and check us to make sure we were OK. Everyone survived the calamity except the janitor. He got fired.

We were no longer allowed to use the fire escape for recess, but I kept drawing pictures for Mrs. Carry, my savior.

Measles and Mumps

Last year I got the measles and this year I caught mumps from some kids at school.

I was in public school. I started feeling bad, and started itching. White and red spots started showing up on my arms. I went to the teacher and told her that I thought I was getting measles. Some of the other kids had already had them. She told me to pull up my shirt. She checked my belly. "Yes," she said, "you have measles."

She told me get my books and took me to the coatroom. "Stay here until school lets out for the day." Then I could get on the school bus to go home. Kids who lived in town were excused to go home if they got sick, but those of us who rode the bus had to wait, unless our parents could come to school and get us. It was already about 2:00 when my measles broke out, so the teacher told me to wait (my folks did not have a car to come for me anyway).

There was only one small light bulb in the ceiling. There were no windows. The coatroom was used for more than just hanging coats. It was also a room for students to be placed in when they behaved badly, and it was used to keep sick kids like me away from the other students.

Finally, I heard the bell ring. All the kids started leaving to go home. The teacher came and walked me to my school bus. She told Mr. Lackey that I had measles. He told me to go sit in the last row of seats. He told the other kids to stay close to the front of the bus. For the first time, I realized how the colored must feel when the bus driver told them to go to the back of the bus.

My ride home was miserable; I had a fever and was itching. Momma was still at work and Daddy was in town, so the only thing I knew to do was walk down to Fricky Johnson's house. Kenny was with me. He said, "Fricky will know what to do. She always does."

I could tell that she was not happy to have me come to her house because now Johnny and Sally would get measles too. She felt sorry for me and told me to come in. She said, "My kids will probably get it, anyway." She had me lay down on the bed. She said she was going to treat me with her country medicine ways. She took a small pinch of new snuff from her little snuff-can and put it into some warm water and stirred it. She said, "I have never tried tobacco juice on measles before, but it works on bee stings, so maybe it will work on measles too." Then she took a cloth and gently rubbed the thin warm snuff mixture all over the measles spots. It burned a bit at first, but then the itching got better. Then she took talcum power and rubbed over my body.

A little later, when Momma got home, she wondered where Kenny and I were. She went to Fricky's house and found Kenny and me there. She thanked Fricky and then walked us home. The next few days I was pretty sick, but survived. After a week at home, I went back to school.

That was last year, and now I caught the mumps. This year I was back in church school. It was a single one-room school in the back of the church building. There was no coatroom for the teacher to put me in to keep me away from the other kids, so she had to put me in the church meeting room and I had to wait there until I could go home. At least there were windows, unlike the coatroom.

Most days, Kenny and I rode back and forth to school with the Nash family in their car. When Mrs. Nash came to school to pick us up to carry us home, she discovered that I had the mumps. She got concerned and told me to sit in the back seat of the car. She had the other four kids all pile in the front seat with her. I thought that was a bit crazy to keep us separated with only one seat separating us. I had spent the whole day with the kids and we all touched the same things. Now I had to sit in the "back of the bus" again.

Since Momma was not yet home from work, I thought I should ask Mrs. Nash to drop us off at Fricky's house, but Kenny said this year he thought he was old enough to take care of me until Momma got home. This was probably best because the mumps are inside your body and Fricky might have had me swallow snuff as her country cure.

Kenny did a good job. I was miserable, so he kept wiping my face with a wet cloth. Both sides of my neck and jaws swelled up and I had a fever. The pain in the jaws was terrible. Kenny went to the medicine cabinet and brought me two aspirins. They helped.

Finally Momma got home and came to check on me. She told Kenny that he had done a good job as a doctor. He grinned.

Momma said, "You have to stay in bed and be still and quiet so the mumps will not go down on you." I did not understand the "going down on" me thing. Guess it was one of those things only adults talk about.

I stayed in bed, was still and quiet and again survived my terrible disease. It is not easy being a kid and having to go through these "childhood diseases" as they call them. Maybe someday they will figure out a way to keep kids from having to go through all this pain, especially if the mumps go down on them.

Kenny was lucky. He did not get the mumps.

MY RELIGIOUS UPBRINGING

As a child I experienced many traditions of the South including Christian fundamentalist teachings. The South is inundated with a large number of very conservative churches.

My mother was converted to the Seventh-day Adventist religion before I was born. It is even more conservative than many fundamentalist ones. My father did not belong to any religion.

So you could say I was from an "unequally yoked" marriage.

My mother prayed for my soul, my Father did not pray.

Momma Loved Her Church

My Momma loved her little church. It gave her some renewed confidence that somehow, some day, things would look brighter for her.

She paid a faithful tithe; ten percent of her small wages went to the church plus her regular offerings. She made fifteen dollars a week keeping house for people in town. Before she spent a penny of her earnings, she took a dollar and fifty cents and put it in a drawer until time to go to church.

She was the head Deaconess of the church, which meant she was responsible for a number of things. She felt that the most important part of her job was preparing the Communion Service. It was held quarterly, four times a year. Not only did the church members eat bread representing Christ's body and drink his blood (grape juice), but foot washing was an essential part of the ceremony. It taught humility.

This meant Momma had to go to the church on Friday afternoon and put nice wash pans, towels and buckets of water in two separate rooms, one for the men and one for the women. I always went to help her.

She also had to bake unleavened bread to serve, and she had to buy the Welch's Grape Juice (the Adventist church and many other fundamentalist churches believe that Jesus served grape juice at the Last Supper, as wine was something Christians did not drink). We had to pour the grape juice into the tiny little clear glasses that sat in round trays. These would be served to the congregation. I loved the pouring part.

After the Communion was over, and everyone had gone home, Momma and I would have to clean everything. That meant washing all the pans where people's feet were bathed, and putting all the pans and buckets away. We had to take the towels home to wash in our outdoor hand-operated washer.

There was always some bread and grape juice left over after the service. I told Momma that I wanted to eat the bread and drink the juice (I was not old enough to participate in the communion service, as I was not yet baptized. A child needed to wait until they were twelve years old to receive baptism). Momma got a very worried look on her face. She said, "Clydie, this is sacred, and we are supposed to burn the leftover bread and pour out the leftover grape juice."

I looked at Momma for a minute, then I said, "We do not have enough money to drink Welch's Grape Juice at home, and I do not believe that the Lord is going to strike me dead with lightning if I drink it." I could see that she was not sure what she should say. I said, "I think the good Lord would consider it a sin to waste good Welch's Grape Juice. I am going to drink it and if he wants to strike me dead, then that will be the last grape juice for me."

She watched as I took each of the five little glasses that were left and drank them, one at a time. I drank all five and I was still standing. She had a look of relief on her face. I smiled at her and said, "Momma, let's hope that the Lord is too good to strike down a poor boy from Shady Grove Road for drinking a little juice."

We cleaned up and headed for home. I was not sure how she would have explained to the newspaper reporter if I had been struck dead drinking Welch's Grape Juice.

Daddy, Uncle Judd, the Southern Evangelist, Baptism, and the Snake

Summer in the South was hot, "Southern Un-Comfort," my Daddy called it. It was hotter in the South for the poor who did not have electric fans like the rich people. We did not have electric fans in our little house on Shady Grove Road. We were poor, or *a little short on money*, as Daddy always said. The Second World War had ended, and the people were searching for ways to better their lives.

It was steamy July. I was ten years old. Momma told me that our church asked an evangelist to come to our little town and hold tent revival meetings. The church was small and hoped to increase the size of its membership. The members thought this would be the best way to do it.

The day came when the evangelist was to arrive. I rode my bike to the site for the tent and was very excited as I saw him pull up in a large flatbed truck. He was driving and there were three men with him. I introduced myself and told him that my Momma belonged to the church that had asked him to come and preach.

He shook my hand and said, "My name is Brother Bill Davenport and I am glad to meet you, son. I could use your help."

I said, "Just let me know what I can do, sir." I saw streams of sweat flowing down his face. He was a thin, good-looking man with a big smile. To me, he was awful nice looking for being a preacher. I thought the people who came to his revival would really like him. Then he called out orders to the men to unload and pitch the large tent.

I hung around and asked him a thousand questions about his tent and the meetings. He said he was going to hold nightly revival meetings to bring local non-believers into the church. He flashed a big smile and said, "My plan is to get as many people as I can to come to my meetings. I hope they will bring big free-will offerings each night." Then he added, "Of course, at the end of the meetings, I hope to have a lot of people accept Jesus and be baptized."

"Are you going to advertise your meetings in the town newspaper?" I asked.

"No, I have a better plan," he said. "I am going to do two things: I am going to run an ad during the local morning radio *Country Music Show* and I am going to circulate flyers to people's homes to announce that I am going to give away free Bibles. Everyone loves to get a free gift. The free Bible will entice the people to come to the meetings and they will bring their offerings!"

He got very excited and flashed another of his big smiles as he told me this. I watched beads of sweat form on his forehead. "Is there a river nearby where I can baptize the newly expected converts?" "Yes, sir," I told him. "I know the perfect spot. It's a place where we love to swim and the water is clear and peaceful."

He asked if I would go house to house and leave flyers on people's doors inviting them to his evangelistic meetings. The flyers read:

> *FREE BIBLES*
> *Come Sing, Praise the Lord and go home with a <u>free</u>*
>   *Bible*
> *Sunday Night at 7:00 pm*
> *The Big Revival Tent on the Little Rock Highway.*

He handed me several bundles of flyers and I spent the rest of the day going house to house putting the flyers in people's screen doors.

The July heat got even hotter and more humid as I trudged to each home.

I was sweating head to toe when, late that afternoon, I returned and told the preacher that I had placed two hundred flyers on people's doors. He said, "Great, I will pay you a penny for each flyer you distributed." That amounted to two dollars! I could hardly catch my breath as he counted out eight shiny silver quarters. Man! That was a lot of cash! Even one quarter was a lot of money, enough to buy three candy bars and two cold drinks!

He sat down on the bed of his truck, wiped his forehead and continued to tell me his great plan. On opening night, he would give everyone a brand-new genuine imitation leather-bound red-lettered edition of the Bible. Every word that Jesus had spoken was printed in red ink. For the poor in our town, this Bible giveaway would have real appeal. "On the first night," he said, flashing another of his big smiles, "I will present each person attending their own Bible and tell them to write their name in the front. This will let them know the Bible will be theirs to keep. I will explain to them that at the end of each nightly meeting, they will have to return their Bible before they leave to go home."

He explained that each person would be given their Bibles every night when they returned, in order to follow the texts being read. "At the end of the five nights of preaching, each will get to take their Bible home, to keep, but only if they have attended at least four of the five meetings."

After I spent the whole day working for the evangelist, I headed for home and told Daddy and Uncle Judd about the free Bibles and the nice evangelist. Neither of them had an education beyond grade school, but they could read. Their big eyes told me they wanted one of those free Bibles. They both said that they would attend the meetings.

Momma and Aunt Ola already belonged to the church. Daddy and Uncle Judd did not. Momma and Aunt Ola were so happy that their husbands were going to attend the meetings. For years they had prayed their men would join the church.

On opening night a crowd of people gathered at the tent door. They waited in line to be greeted personally by the evangelist and receive their own Bible and a free paper fan. Daddy and Uncle Judd were first in line. They planned to attend all five nights of meetings. On the last night they would each get their free Bible to take home. This offer was only for non-believers who had not yet joined the church. Since Momma and Aunt Ola were already members, they were not eligible.

The evangelist spent each night of the week preaching about a lot of terrible things that would be happening to the earth, including floods and famines and earthquakes, and he ended the week telling about the horrible Armageddon that was coming upon us.

On the closing night the weather was the hottest it had been all week. Everyone was sweating and fanning themselves with the free beautiful paper fans the Ashby Funeral Home had donated. The fans had a picture of Jesus holding a lamb on the front side and "Compliments of Ashby Funeral Home. Prepare to meet Jesus" on the back.

The preacher had the congregation sing *"Just As I Am"* and he called for the spirit to come down on the sinners and help them get out of their seats and come to the front of the tent and publicly accept Jesus before it was too late. I sat between Momma and Aunt Ola and watched their sweating lips move as they silently prayed for the spirit to jolt Daddy and Uncle Judd from their seats and move them to go to the front.

Finally Daddy, Uncle Judd and four others made their way to the preacher, Bibles in hand. The preacher tried to smile but I could see by his face that he had hoped more would respond to his call to come forward and accept Jesus.

The preacher prayed and prayed for the six to accept Jesus, and before long he had talked all six non-believers into being baptized into the church. Momma and Aunt Ola quietly said, "Praise the Lord!"

The baptism was set for Sunday afternoon at 3:00 at our favorite swimming hole in the Saline River, at Cecil Jones's Landing on the Hot Springs Highway.

The church members all gathered on the bank of the slow-flowing river. The preacher brought white robes for those being baptized and they put them on over their clothes.

While the congregation sang hymns, the preacher waded out to where the water was about three feet deep. He had the new converts wade in after him.

The first to be baptized was Mrs. Snork. The preacher completely dunked her under water and she came up waving her arms praising

Jesus. Next was Mr. Reynolds, well known in town as a wayward, unemployed drunk. The preacher did the same as he had with Mrs. Snork. Mr. Reynolds seemed a little embarrassed as he came sputtering up from the water, but he waved his arms too. After the next two were dunked, it was time for Daddy and Uncle Judd. They started wading towards the preacher. The preacher gave them his big smile. Momma and Aunt Ola watched and were so pleased this was happening. "Praise Jesus," they quietly said.

But their quiet moment of victory was shattered when someone yelled, "SNAKE!" Everyone stared in disbelief as a three-foot-long water moccasin slid off the far bank and made his way through the clear water, swimming ever closer to the sinners.

Daddy and Uncle Judd's eyes got as big as saucers. They were scared to death of snakes. They looked at each other, and headed for the near riverbank so fast that you could say they almost walked on water. They beat everybody out. Once on the bank, they pulled off their white robes and dropped them on the ground.

Daddy said, "This is a sign! That snake represents the Devil! He is like the snake that tempted Eve in the Garden of Eden. This means that Jesus is not ready for us yet!" Uncle Judd shook his head in agreement and said, "Amen."

The preacher was momentarily dumbstruck! Then he found his words and sternly said, "This is just that mean old Devil trying to get you men to not accept Jesus!"

Daddy was a superstitious man and said, "I think the Devil is in the snake, and I am not going to get baptized only to be bitten by a poisonous water moccasin in the river and die. I would rather be a live sinner than a dead saint!" Daddy and Uncle Judd never did get baptized, but they did keep their genuine imitation leather, red-lettered edition of the Bible. It made them proud. They knew that most poor people were not lucky enough to have a red-lettered edition of the Bible to proudly display in the living room next to the lamp with the original cellophane covering over the lampshade.

The next day, I again rode my bike down to the tent site and watched as the preacher supervised the folding and packing of his tent onto the flatbed truck. It was still hot and he was still sweating. He did not have much to say to me.

I was not sure he had done that well financially with his evangelistic meetings. He had given away about forty Bibles, paid for a radio ad, paid me to hand out flyers and yet had only won four souls into the church. I was sure that the free-will offerings he requested each night did not amount to much. Being only ten years old, I was sure I did not know a lot, but if I were the preacher, I think I might consider selling used cars, or life insurance policies, or even burial insurance for the Ashby Funeral Home.

As I watched the preacher's truck pull onto the highway, I waved goodbye to him. I had hoped that, before leaving, he might give me one of those beautiful genuine imitation leather, red-lettered editions of the Bible. But he didn't. He didn't even smile. He just waved as the truck disappeared down the Little Rock Highway.

Adam and Eve

Sometimes I made teachers feel uncomfortable when I didn't mean to, especially in church and in church school. I had a lot of questions that I would liked to have had answered.

When I was in fifth grade, we again had church school.

Kenny and I were yo-yoed back and forth; one year in public school and the next in church school. Our Mommas thought we should be in church school whenever possible.

The church had a one-room school with grades one through eight. There were usually about 10-12 students in the whole school. It was very small.

Bible classes were taught to all eight grades at once. I always seemed to be the oldest in the classes. Miss Snow, who was white as snow including her white hair, was our teacher.

During the Bible class, she told us the story of Creation, the Garden of Eden, and about Adam and Eve being the first people on earth. She said, "God made Adam, then made him a helpmate." I assumed she meant wife. Then she said, "Adam and Eve had two sons, Cain and Abel and they all started the human race."

She showed us artist's paintings of Adam and Eve standing behind bushes, or sometimes Adam would have a little leaf that covered his thing and Eve would have three little leaves covering her three things.

I asked Miss Snow, "What happens when Adam and Eve go out in the hot sun and their leaves start to shrivel." She got flustered and did not know what to say. Finally she came up with a lame idea that they had to pull some new leaves quick. I accepted that answer, but the thought crossed my mind that it would be funny if they picked poison ivy instead of Oak or Maple.

Then I asked Miss Snow if Adam and Eve had more kids, possibly some girls too. She said, "Yes, I am sure they did."

So I asked her if Eve *did it* with her sons and Adam *did it* with his daughters in order to increase the human race, or did the sons and the daughters *do it* together to make more kids.

Miss Snow turned summer red; She did not know what to say. I was not sure if she knew what I meant by *doing it*, because she had never had any kids, therefore she had never *done it*.

She started telling me, "You should not doubt the Bible, and you just need to have more faith in the Bible." I did not doubt the Bible, but the way some good people interpreted it.

I had lots of doubts, but one thing I did not doubt was that I could sneak a kiss from Susie Jones, as we walked through the woods on the way home from school.

Susie's Momma always told her to never stop in the woods, to always keep walking. It was difficult to sneak a kiss while walking, but we mastered it. I never did understand the *not stopping* thing.

Mommas could be strange.

Prayer Meetings

Our little church always had Prayer Meetings on Wednesday nights. Momma made Kenny and me go. We would all meet in the small white wooden church, sing a few songs and then everyone would get down on their knees. Everyone was invited to pray out loud, one at a time. Everyone, with eyes closed.

The prayer thing would go on forever, or at least thirty minutes. Kenny and I were bored to death. We thought the prayers would never end. The good people would pray for the sick and shut-ins, pray for the missionaries in the foreign field, pray for rain for the corn in the farmer's fields. Some would pray for the backsliders in the church who had lost their way, or for sister Thomas' daughter, who for some reason had to move to another town for a few months.

In order for Kenny and me to survive the pain of these weekly meetings, we had to do something different. We would get down on our knees with the rest of the people, but we would take a songbook down with us. We would turn the pages and whisper the titles of the songs. We would add the words Under the Bed to each title. He Walks with Me and He Talks with Me Under the Bed, On a Hill Far Away Stands the Old Rugged Cross Under the Bed, or In the Sweet By and By Under the Bed.

We would get tickled and try not to laugh, but the more we tried not to laugh, the worse it got. If a laugh slipped out, we would try to act like we were coughing to cover our laugh.

Brother Britt, the head elder of the church, who stuttered, would hear us and then he would start to pray for the way-way-way-ward chi-chi-children. This usually brought the prayer meeting to an end. We always thought it would be funny for one of us to pray for the prayers to end, but we would probably burn in hell for an eternity for that one.

We did not do that prayer.

Noah's Ark

It was raining hard, really hard and had been for days. Daddy said, "We had better start building an ark." I knew he was teasing. I said, "Noah had to saw a lot of lumber to build such a large boat. It had to be big enough to hold two of every animal on earth."

Daddy looked at me and said he was not sure he believed that story. I said, "Oh, yes, the teacher at church told me." He said, "Ask your teacher why Noah did not take any dinosaurs into the ark. I am sure God made them, too."

The next time I was at church, I asked the teacher about the dinosaurs. She was not sure what to say. She said, "Well, the dinosaurs were very large and there was not enough room on the boat for them." I wanted to know, too, if he took poisonous snakes on the boat.

I said, "That does not seem fair. Just because something is large, does not mean that it should not get a place on the boat. Noah *could* have taken baby dinosaurs, because they were smaller. After all, think about how tall a giraffe is, and how big an elephant is. Why did he make room for those dumb poisonous snakes?"

I continued, "If the whole earth was covered with water, then every person and every other living creature except Noah, his family and the animals he chose had to die. That means Noah and his wife and kids had to start to populate the earth again. This is just like starting the Garden of Eden thing all over again."

She could see that I was having problems with her answers. She said, "You should talk to the preacher about this. He went to school to learn how to answer hard questions like these."

I did not ask the preacher. I think he had enough to do just trying to convert sinners into the church, and then to keep them there.

I went home and told Daddy that I did not get good answers about Noah and the boat thing. He just looked at me, spit some tobacco juice into his can and said, "Son, maybe there just ain't answers for some things, that is what makes the world go round."

I was not sure what he meant by that. I guessed I just needed to have faith. I was fooled by the story of the "Stork Brings Babies" thing when I was seven years old, then about "The Santa Thing" until I was eight years old and now I was not sure that old Noah saved everything he could have saved. Now I was ten years old and needed some good answers.

Raptured

One Sunday morning, the Johnsons decided to go to Sunday school. They stopped by our house and asked Kenny and me if we wanted to go. We did. We piled into the back of Gus Johnson's old Model A Ford pickup with Johnny and his sister Sally. She always sat by me.

In church, the pastor preached that someday the Lord would come and that only the good Baptist people who had been born again would be secretly raptured and taken away swiftly just like that, leaving the others behind. That sounded kind of scary to me. He said people would discover their neighbors missing.

I got to thinking about this. I didn't think the preacher's idea would include Kenny and me, as we were not Baptists. I guessed Johnny and Sally were lucky, since they claimed to be Baptists.

If Baptists were raptured, taken away, that would leave those people's houses and cars without owners. Maybe that way Kenny and I could get a house and car for our parents for free.

I just hoped that when the good Baptist people got raptured, they would leave the house and car keys where we could find them.

After church, we could not wait to get home and tell Momma and Daddy our newfound idea.

Heaven, Not Today

At church, Kenny and I were taught that we should all want to go to heaven, and not to Hell. Hell was a hot and miserable place where you burned forever. I could not really understand the burn forever part. But, they said, heaven was a beautiful place with streets paved in gold, and doorknobs made of diamonds. I could not really understand that. It sounded awfully glitzy to me. I liked hills and creeks and sand and dirt and ponds to skinny-dip in. Heaven sounded boring to me.

I wondered who could read this in the Bible and then want to go to such a place where you would need to wear sunglasses each day, just to see.

I had asked the teachers about love and marriage in heaven. Would people grow old there? Would you have kids there? The teachers said, "Well, we think that all the people will just be kind of the same. Maybe we will all be like angels, neither men or women".

This certainly did not make me very excited about heaven. This was not what I had hoped heaven was about.

They also told us that someday soon, Christ would return to earth to gather his people and take them to heaven to be with him. They said that the Bible says, "He will come in the sky in a cloud and it will be about the size of a man's hand at first, then get larger as he nears the earth."

The next day, Kenny and I were walking up Shady Grove Road kicking sand and talking about this heaven business. Neither of us was too keen on the idea. We liked where we lived, we just wished we had a little more money and running water in our houses, and an indoor toilet.

As we were talking, I looked up in the sky and there, away off in the distance, was a small white cloud, about the size of a man's hand. I grabbed Kenny, and said, "Look, Kenny, I think the Lord is coming!" It scared us both to death. What if we were not ready? What if we had some evil thoughts in our brains, or hearts, as the church called it?

I said to Kenny, "I am not ready to go to Heaven, I want to get married first, be able to *do it* with my wife and have some kids. You will never be able to *do it* in Heaven!" Kenny was only eight years old and was not sure what I meant by *"doing it."*

I did not know what to do. I told Kenny to hide with me under some bushes nearby. We did. We watched the cloud. It started getting bigger, and then all of a sudden, it disappeared. Gone. I grabbed Kenny, and said, "Boy that was a close call." I was so relieved.

Then we went down the road and went skinny-dipping in Mr. Gerard's pond. We needed a break. This had been a very heavy day. We were not ready for heaven, not today.

Frank Paulson's Funeral

The Paulsons were neighbors who lived on Shady Grove Road about half a mile from us. They were a family of six with two boys and two girls. The boys were both older than me. Jenny and Marty were nearer my age. They were good church-going Baptist people.

Their oldest son Frank graduated from Benton High School last year. He got a good job driving a Euclid Truck. We called the trucks Euks. They were huge, with the tires on them being taller than a grown man. The Alcoa Aluminum and the Reynolds Aluminum companies used the trucks for moving ore at the bauxite mines near our home.

One day, the Paulsons got a horrible telephone call on the telephone party line. Many neighbors picked up their phones and listened in on the conversation. It was news that Frank's Euk had turned over and rolled down into the mine. He was seriously hurt and the company was taking him to the hospital in Little Rock.

We all hung up our party line phones in disbelief. Soon, I heard the Ashby Funeral Home ambulance shrieking towards Little Rock. We all knew that it was taking Frank to the hospital.

Within the next few hours, someone called on the party line and we all learned that Frank had died. The community was shocked and terribly saddened.

A few days later the funeral was held at the Oak Grove Missionary Baptist Church, a couple of miles from our house. Everyone went.

Ashby Funeral Home was in charge of the service. Daddy said we had better get to the church early if we wanted a seat. We arrived early and took a seat in the second row. The first row was reserved for the family.

When we arrived, the casket was already there. It was open for people to pass by and see Frank for the last time. Momma asked Kenny and me if we wanted to walk past and see Frank. We were not sure. We had not been to a funeral before, but we decided to go past the casket. We looked and hurried back to our seats. We did not like looking at a dead person.

In a few minutes, the family was ushered into the church. Two men had to practically carry Mrs. Paulson in. Everyone was weeping. As the preacher started preaching and saying nice things about Frank, the crying got louder. Before long the whole church was crying out loud.

Jerry, Frank's younger brother, was beside himself. He ran up to the casket, right during the preaching, and tried to either get into the casket, or pull his brother out of the casket. We could not tell for sure what he was trying to do. Two men had to restrain him. It was terrifying for Kenny and me.

It was so sad for Jerry, Jenny and Marty. We felt so badly for them.

The service was finally over. Everyone drove to the cemetery. Again everybody started weeping and wailing. It was so sadly terrible.

The next day, Kenny and I picked a bunch of wild flowers and took them to Jenny and Marty. We left the flowers at the door with a little note saying we were so sorry. We did not knock; we just left them there. We could not stand to see Jenny and Marty crying again.

The New Country Church

Kenny and I watched a group of men working on a new building. It was on Mr. Winger's property, near our house on Congo Road. They worked on it for days. Everyone wondered what it was going to be. No one asked. They did not want to snoop. Someone asked Mr. Winger. He said he did not know. He simply sold them an acre of land.

Every few days, we would ride our bikes over to watch. Daddy had told us not to be asking the men questions.

One day we rode over. They were putting a steeple on top of the roof. We decided it was time for someone to ask about this new building. We had waited long enough. I asked.

One of the men told me it was going to be a Pentecostal Church. We did not know what that meant.

We rode home and told Daddy that we heard someone say the new building was going to be a Pentecostal Church. His eyes got big! He said, "Those are what they call Holy Rollers." I said, "What does Holy Roller mean?"

He paused for a time, and then said, "They do strange things during church. They pray in 'tongues,' jump up and down, run up and down the aisle and get down on the floor and ROLL! That is why people call them Holy Rollers." I said, "Are they dangerous?" Daddy said he did not think so, but warned us not to go near when they had a church service, either day or night. Kenny got a strange frightened look on his face. He liked to pray, but he was not going for this rolling thing.

A few weeks later the church was finally finished. We had almost forgotten about it. One night, at dusk, we told Momma and Daddy that we wanted to walk up to Congo Road and watch the flying bats. Shady Grove Road was sandy, but Congo Road was gravel. We would pick up a hand full of gravel and throw it into the air and watch the bats chase the gravel as it fell back to earth. We did not hurt the bats, but we got a kick out of making them think they were chasing bugs as they dove down right over our heads.

We were having a blast. Suddenly we heard what we thought was a scream, and then we heard yelling in a strange language. We looked at each other and started to run home. I suddenly realized, that this must be the Holy Rollers having their first church service. I finally convinced Kenny to come with me to have a look. He said, "Are you sure we won't get killed?" I said, "No, they love Jesus." He said, "We do too, but we are not dangerous."

We went over the hill. We could see the lights burning through the open windows and door. We got on our bellies and started to crawl through the tall grass towards the church until we were getting close to the building. Kenny said, "Whoa, I am not getting any closer. They might roll right out here."

We watched through the open door. They spoke in tongues, they clapped, they hollered and some of them got down on the floor and rolled, just like Daddy said they would do. Two of the church members took a small boy and sat him in the aisle, with one of them on each side. They clapped together over his head. I don't know what he had done to deserve this, but he must have been a very bad boy. That scared us the most.

We had enough for one night. We were a bit spooked. We headed for home, but we did keep looking over our shoulder.

When we entered the house, Daddy said, "Were the bats exciting?" We said, "Oh, yes, very exciting."

We never did tell Daddy what really excited us that night. I did not want to get a whipping. Kenny's Momma would have given him one too. We kept our mouths shut and never spoke of the Holy Rollers again.

The Nuns

The South had lots of born-again conservative churches. There were very few Catholic churches. A lot of the good Baptists say, "Stay away from them, they are evil." At least that was what some of the Baptists kids told us.

We were curious about the Catholics. One day Kenny and I rode our bikes on the street that had the only Catholic Church in town. It was called "Our Lady of Fatima." We had no idea what that meant. As we neared the church, two nuns came out and started walking towards us. They had long black dresses that hung all the way to the sidewalk. They had a head thing that only showed a small part of their faces.

Kenny said, "I think they do look like the Devil." I said, "The Devil does not look like that; He is red with horns." We were scared but we were not going to look like cowards, so we just sat on our bikes in the street.

As they got nearer, we tried to see if we could get a glimpse under their head covering. Some Baptist kids had told us that the nuns shaved their heads, and that they did not have one hair on their head. We could not see under the head cloth. We thought we should not get any closer to look.

They saw us watching them. One of them said, "Hello boys. It is a beautiful day, isn't it?" We said, "Yes, ma'am, in fact it is hot today, above ninety degrees." We were trying to sound grown-up. We had said enough. We said no more.

We started to pedal back home. We had seen our first nuns. They had not appeared evil, or looked like the Devil.

We wanted to find those Baptists kids and tell them that we had talked to some nuns, up really close, and we had survived.

OUR TOWN

My hometown, Benton, Arkansas, is situated about half way between Little Rock and Hot Springs. When I was a boy in the 1940s and 50s it had a square block in town where the major stores were located. We had no shopping malls. Downtown, as we called it, was the place to be, especially on Saturday, day or night. No stores were ever open on Sundays.

There was no hospital, no department store and no bars. Our county was dry, so stores were not allowed to sell liquor, wine or beer. The people of our town had to drive to the county line to purchase the Devil's brew, as some of the good Baptists called it.

Mr. Gingles, the only Jew in town according to Daddy, owned most of the stores in town. Our favorite was Gingles Shoe Store, where he had a fluoroscope x-ray machine that we kids would use every Saturday night. We would look down into it to see the bones in our feet as we wiggled our toes. No one had any idea that x-rays were dangerous.

We had two movie theaters in town that showed the latest Tom Mix and Hopalong Cassidy movies. What more could a boy want.

Western Auto Store

One of Kenny and my favorite things to do was to ride our bikes into town to visit the Western Auto Store. It was the store that also sold bicycles. When you opened the front door you could smell fresh rubber tires on the new bicycles. We knew we would never have the money for new bikes, but we did love to look and dream.

The store had a good selection of Western Flyers, the store brand. They also had a few Schwinn bikes that were made in Germany–at least that is what we were told.

We always had money with us when we rode our bikes to town. We had been saving from the sale of cold drink bottles. We looked at all the bike accessories: reflectors, mud flaps, bells, battery-operated horns and handlebar grips.

As we entered the store we discovered something new: The 3M Company had come out with red reflective tape that you could buy in small pieces. These could be stuck on bike fenders so that they glowed when car lights shined on your bike at night. The reflector tape would keep us safe if we could ever ride our bikes at night on the roads around our house. We bought the reflective tape, some other reflectors and a battery-operated light for each of our bikes. We headed for home, feeling proud.

Since our bikes were older, we repainted them once or twice each summer. When we got home, we cleaned our bikes and painted them a new color. We had to wait until the next day before the paint dried enough to apply the new reflective tape.

The next day we carefully applied the tape, drilled new holes for the other reflectors and attached our new handlebar headlights. Daddy watched us do this and said, "When it gets dark, I will bring my big flashlight and shine it on your new reflective tape." This one time he said that we could ride on the road at night. He shined his flashlight and yelled, "Yes, the two of you do glow." We were so happy. Then Daddy said, "When you are ten years old, you can start riding on the road at night."

Dry County

Saline County was my county and it was dry. That meant that the good Southern Christian people of my county did not want any kind of liquor, wine or beer to be sold there, as it is the "Devil's drink." We lived about seven miles from the Pulaski County line where they did sell the "evil stuff."

What Kenny and I did notice was that every Friday evening, after work, we saw a lot of cars heading up that way. In about half an hour we saw the same cars coming back towards home.

We often wonder if they brought the liquor back to their Christian homes and drank it while they sat on the sofa under the beautiful blue cardboard sign that said, *Jesus Lives in This House.*

Distant Ambulance in the Night

Summer nights were unbearably hot. I lay awake in my bed, sweated and wished we had a fan in our house. The windows were all open. There was no breeze to move the curtains. I heard the whippoorwill singing in the night. I wondered if she, or he, was as hot and sweaty as I was. I knew I didn't feel like singing.

I lay there trying to go to sleep. In the distance I heard the night train crawling its way through our county. I heard it giving its long whistle blast at each road crossing.

As I listened, I heard the Ashby Funeral Home ambulance shrieking over the night highway toward Little Rock. We did not have a hospital in my hometown. I imagined a car wreck with people being killed, or someone being burned in a house fire or many other horrible possibilities. I never thought of someone having a heart attack, or someone rich falling in their big bathtubs and breaking a hip or something. The screaming Ashby ambulance told me something terrible had taken place.

The siren faded away. I finally fell asleep

The next morning we listened to the local radio station. The newsman announced the price of hogs and grain in Chicago and the local weather. Hot. He said, "The Ashby Funeral Home ambulance took Mrs. Archie Smith to the Baptist Hospital in Little Rock last night to deliver twins, a boy and a girl."

Then he said, "The ambulance was also able to attend to an overturned car on its return from Little Rock. A man from Benton, returning from the county line, was killed in the wreck. Ashby Funeral Home will announce calling hours for the man on tomorrow's news."

The next night when I went to my sweaty bed, I listened for the train, the whippoorwill and Ashby's ambulance and wondered if they would pick up business going both ways.

Maybe when I grow up I will want to be an ambulance driver. I wondered if they got tips for good service.

Lightning Storms

In the spring and fall we have great lightning and thunderstorms. I love the storms at night because the lightning always brings the rain. There is nothing as exciting as hearing heavy raindrops hammering the tin roof of our house. When the lightning strikes it makes a terrific boom and it lights up my room like it is daylight. As soon as the lightning strikes, I count 1001, 1002, 1003 to see how far away it hits something. One night it hit the large pine tree just down Shady Grove Road.

I did not even get to 1001 before I heard a tree cracking and breaking to the ground. This was the third time this same tree has been hit by lightning.

Fricky Johnson says the tree is cursed. I say if I were a squirrel, I would look for a shorter tree to build my nest.

Swimming in the Town Pool

In the fourth grade, I made a new friend. His name was Ronnie Watson. He lived in town in a nice house.

One summer day I was in town on my bike and I went by to see him. We played in his yard. He asked me, "Would you like to go swimming in the town swimming pool?"

I told him that I had never been in a town pool. I only swam in rivers and lakes. He said I was in for a surprise. I told him I did not have any swim trunks with me. He said he had an extra pair I could use.

We went to the pool, only a few blocks from his house. I did not know you had to pay twenty-five cents to get into the pool. I had fifteen cents in my pocket. Ronnie said he would loan me a dime. We went into a locker room to change clothes. The sign said, "Shower before entering Pool." I thought this was strange, because you were going to get wet in the pool. Why shower now?

Ronnie said, "Just do it, so we can go in." We put our clothes in a basket and put them in a locker. We took the required shower, removed the key from the locker and pinned it to our trunks.

As we walked out to the pool, what I saw seemed unbelievable to me. The water was so clear that I could see the bottom. I could see everyone swimming underwater. The thought hit me, "You cannot pee in this clear water because people will see the yellow water surrounding you. You have to get out of the water and go into the bathhouse to pee." What a waste of time. So, I did not pee in the water as we did when we swam in the rivers and lakes.

I found that I could go under water, open my eyes and see everything, including the pretty girl's legs. The chlorine in the water hurt my eyes. Hurt or not, I kept my eyes open under the water.

After a couple of hours, we went back into the shower room to get ready to go home. Ronnie said, "Now we take a shower, again." Strange, I thought. We have been in the water for two hours. Do we really need a shower? There are some things that the city people do that just don't make sense in the real world.

My Community

Our community was made up of about a dozen homes, spread apart. There were no houses next to each other, like you would find in town. It was basically two miles of Shady Grove Road and about two miles of Congo Road. The roads crossed right at our house.

There was the Missionary Baptist Church at one end of the community and there was a new Pentecostal Church near our house (although the community members did not consider it a part of our community, as its members were from away, possibly from in town. No one ever asked them).

There were no stores, no community hall and not even a Mom and Pop's grocery. There were just several very poor families, and a few families who lived above the poverty line.

About the only time the families got together socially was for a Halloween party for the kids, or for a funeral. The families pretty much stayed to themselves, unless there was a calamity, then everyone pitched in.

The Automobile Accident on Congo Road

When I was six years old, Momma and I saw a terrible automobile accident on Congo Road.

Momma had just told me that we were going to walk to Mrs. Paulson's house to borrow some flour. We walked up Shady Grove Road and were about to cross Congo Road when I heard a car coming really fast. I told Momma that we had better stay back, because the car seemed to be going much too fast for the gravel road. We got back off the road and watched as the car came flying down the road. We looked in the other direction, and there was a pickup truck coming down the road. We recognized that the truck was my Uncle Judd's truck. He had gone to the Greyhound bus station to pick up my brother, Willy, who was coming home on furlough from the Navy.

My Momma panicked. We saw the car sliding out of control. The pickup truck tried to avoid the other car by driving off the road into the barbed wire fence. But the car slammed into Uncle Judd's truck, then spun across the road and into the other ditch. Everything was silent for a couple of moments.

Momma and I started to run to Uncle Judd's truck. Willy and Uncle Judd were still inside; their heads had hit the windshield. But they were both conscious and starting to climb out of the truck.

Willy said, "Hi, Momma. I have got to try to help the guy in the other car." The guy was not moving. He too had slammed into the windshield of his car. Willy was bleeding. He ran over and pulled the guy out and started doing artificial respiration on him.

Uncle Judd was in a daze, just walking around.

Mrs. Winger, who lived up the road, heard the crash. She came running with some sheets. She started ripping them to make bandages. Someone else had already gone to town to get the ambulance.

Momma started helping Willy attend to the unknown man who had caused the accident. The Ashby Funeral Home ambulance soon arrived. They put the man on a stretcher and into the ambulance. Momma and I also got in, so Momma could try to help him. Uncle Judd and Willy were taken to the hospital in a neighbor's car. Everyone was trying to help.

The ride in the ambulance was exciting and scary with the siren blasting away. The man on the stretcher kept moaning something, but we could not tell what it was he was saying. Momma said he had a strong smell of liquor on his breath. He had probably been up in the hills buying moonshine whisky. Our county was a dry county, but there were men up in the hill country that sold illegal whisky that they made.

The man lived, but suffered brain damage. Willy and Uncle Judd survived but each lost a couple of teeth and had scars. Momma and I survived, but had our wits scared out of us.

We were glad to have Willy home with us for furlough. He said it was a heck of a welcome home. He said he thought he was probably safer at war than being run into by a drunk on Congo Road.

Momma and I never did get the flour from Mrs. Paulson that we were on our way to get. The accident caused us to forget all about baking a cake to welcome Willy home.

The next day we went to the store and bought a bag of flour and made a big cake just for Willy.

Sleepover at the Johnsons' House

My best friend was Johnny Johnson–that is, besides Kenny. Johnny lived just over the hill from us on Shady Grove Road. His family was poorer than we were.

Johnny's Momma was called Fricky–a funny name, I thought. His Daddy was called Gus.

Johnny had some older brothers and sisters. One of his sisters was named Sally. She was three years older than Johnny and me.

Kenny and I spent a lot of time at the Johnson's house.

Fricky was good to us. She wore what they called a rat in her hair. She wrapped her hair around it. One time I saw her with her hair combed out and it was very long. She was also very cross-eyed. Daddy said she was so cross-eyed that when she cried, the tears ran down her back. I thought he was teasing about this, but I had never seen her cry.

Sometimes on Saturdays I spent the night with the Johnsons. Kenny did not stay overnight. He was too young.

Johnny, Sally and I all slept in the same bedroom. Sally slept in one bed and Johnny and me in the other. Sometimes Sally would leave her bed and get in bed between Johnny and me and I liked that. The room was next to where Fricky and Gus slept. Gus snored really loudly. They said I would get used to it.

Gus Johnson did not have a regular job. He had a bad leg and had to use a cane to walk. He somehow got enough money together to buy a very old rusty Model A Ford pickup truck. He went around and picked up things that others threw away, then tried to sell them in front of his house. He made a few dollars, I guessed.

I liked the Johnsons. It was fun to spend Saturday nights with them. We all sat around the radio and listened to the Grand Old Opry. We all tried to sing the songs that we knew with the radio. We really didn't sound that good. Gus had a high-pitched voice, a bit like a rooster crowing. We all laughed but he did not know that it was at him.

Early Sunday morning, Johnny and I awoke early so we could slip into the woods and watch the squirrels playing in the trees. We did not have guns so we tried to hit them with rocks from our slingshots. We made the slingshots out of a Y branch from a tree with pieces of black inner tube rubber and a piece of old leather.

The squirrels were smart. We never hit one. They always outsmarted us. I think they looked forward to us coming down to the woods on Sunday mornings so they could tease us, but we loved it. We laughed a lot and came back to the house about the time the others were getting up.

Fricky made biscuits and poured us each a glass of buttermilk that she had churned. We each got a piece of fried salt pork, white Wonder Bread and imitation honey-flavored syrup. No butter. No coffee.

We ate it like we liked it. I thanked them for letting me spend the night and for a delicious breakfast. Fricky looked and me and said, "Clydie, you are welcome here anytime." Gus said nothing. He just smiled and spit his tobacco juice into an old coffee can.

I told Johnny and Sally goodbye and headed for home for a cup of hot coffee with Daddy.

The Sugar Cane Wagon

I was lying in the hammock we had tied between the oak trees in the front yard. Kenny was on the tire swing.

Kenny said, "I hear a wagon coming up the road." I jumped out of the hammock. There was a team of horses pulling an old farm wagon past our house.

We ran out to the road to meet it. We said, "Hey, what's on the wagon?" The driver said, "It's a load of sugar cane I am taking to the juicer to get made into sorghum." Then he said, "You can each have one cane to chew." We walked behind the wagon for a couple of minutes.

I said to Kenny, "Why don't we get on the wagon and go with him to see how they squeeze the juice out of the cane." Kenny said, "We better ask him where he is going, and how far it is."

Good idea, I thought. So we asked and the man said, "About three miles, I guess."

Our Mommas were at work. Daddy was in town at the Courthouse sitting on the outside benches and spitting tobacco juice with the other old men who had nothing better to do.

We jumped on the wagon; each pulled a piece of sugar cane and started chewing. It was sweet, but kind of watery.

After a while, we got to the place where they were squeezing the cane into juice and boiling it to make sorghum. They had a big sorghum juicer machine in the middle. A mule was hitched to a long pole that attached to the juicer. The mule walked in a circle, round and round. Many times. A man pushed the canes into the teeth of the machine. The juice was squeezed and ran into a pipe that went to the large metal pan over a roaring fire.

Kenny and I watched as it boiled into dark syrup. One of the men skimmed off a tin cup full and brought it over to us. "Watch yourselves and don't burn your tongue. It is hotter'en hell."

We thanked him and let it cool. It was really good. We both loved it.

We were about to leave for home. One of the men asked if our Momma liked sorghum. We said she did. He pulled out a pint jar from under the seat of his truck. It had a small amount of clear liquid in it. He drank the liquid, went over to a barrel of water and rinsed it. Then he filled it with new hot sorghum and said, "Take this to your Momma." That's all he said.

We knew we had three miles to walk home and it was getting late. The old man who gave us the sorghum said, "I am headed down your way in my truck to take the squeezed cane to a farmer to feed his cows. Would you like a ride?"

We said, "Yes'ir, we would appreciate that." He had two other men in the cab of the truck with him. He said we would have to crawl up high onto the load of cane and for us to hold on tight.

We did, the truck bumped, the truck jerked, the truck jolted and we hung on for dear life. Kenny prayed. We were so relieved when the truck finally stopped in front of our house.

We jumped off the truck, and thanked the man. We had lived through another Kenny and Clyde adventure on the little farm on Shady Grove Road.

However, I wished I knew what was in that pint jar before he rinsed it with cold water.

The "Green Valley Traveling Groceries" Bus

One day Kenny and I heard a horn honking. We ran outside to see what it was. There was an old school bus that had been painted green. It had a sign that said "Green Valley Traveling Groceries" on the side.

The man stopped and asked us if we would like to go inside the bus to see what he had for sale. We did, and were we surprised! He had shelves on each side all the way to the back of the bus. He had many kinds of canned goods, flour, sugar and candy too. He then said, "Go get your Momma to come out and see."

By now, Momma and Daddy were both coming out to see what all the commotion was about.

Daddy stayed outside the bus. He did not want to go in. Momma did–she went in and looked over everything. She started to ask questions about prices of different items. As the man started telling her his prices, I could see a frown coming across Momma's face. She said, "Now, that is higher than I pay at Congo Grocery." The man said, "Yes, a bit higher, but I bring it to your door. You can see all the items yourself."

Momma got off the "Green Valley Traveling Groceries" bus. She said, "Sir, I appreciate you being so nice as to stop by our house and offer us your wares. The Congo Grocery truck brings our groceries each week to our door, too, and their prices are better, so we need to stay with them. They have been so good to us."

"Now, before you go on down the road, could I offer you a nice glass of cold sweet tea," she said with a Christian smile on her face.

The man thought for a moment, then said, "Just a moment." He went into the bus and came back with some penny candy for Kenny and me. He gave a big Christian smile and accepted Momma's sweet tea.

Cleaning the Cemetery Lot

On the day before Memorial Day, Fricky Johnson asked me if I wanted to go with her family up to the Congo Village to clean their first daughter's grave. She died when she was a baby.

It was about ten miles and we had to go by horse and wagon. Gus did not yet have the old pickup truck that he was hoping to buy when he saved enough money. I had never been on a long wagon ride before.

The Johnsons ate mustard and sugar sandwiches on white bread. I said I would bring my own sandwich. I did not want mustard and sugar again. I brought a baloney sandwich.

We had a large metal can of water, a large glass jar of red Kool Aid and a bunch of mustard and sugar sandwiches. Mr. Johnson, Fricky, Johnny's momma, Sally, Johnny and I crawled into the wagon at dawn.

The trip was exciting at first, and then the miles started to pass by really slowly. We stopped after about an hour so we could all pee. Fricky and Sally squatted in the bushes and we men went to the other side of the wagon. Johnny and I had a peeing contest to see who could shoot the farthest. I won and Mr. Johnson laughed.

Finally we came to a hill, and the cemetery was just down below. Mr. Johnson got out of the wagon and put a large axe handle through the wooden spokes of one wheel and wedged it into the frame of the wagon. This caused the wagon wheel to slide and not turn. I asked, "Why are you doing this?" He said, "I am making a brake for the wagon so as we go down the steep hill the wagon will not run over the horse." It worked. We made it down the hill.

We were all hungry. We sat on the grass beside the grave and opened our bag lunches. My baloney sandwich smelled strong compared to their sugar and mustard ones. They all watched me unwrap the wax paper from my sandwich. I did not want to watch them unwrap theirs. My sandwich now did not look so good.

I asked Mr. Johnson to loan me his pocketknife. I had watched him skin raccoons with it after a coon hunt. So I knew it was sharp. I cut my two sandwiches into five pieces each and handed a piece to each one. They took the knife and gave me some of their mustard and sugar. No one said anything. We just ate and drank the warm red Kool Aid.

We all raked and cleaned. It was time to climb back into the wagon. We headed back up the steep hill towards home. The horse was old. We all got out of the wagon and pushed the wagon as the horse pulled.

We three kids slept most of the way back. The return trip was much shorter.

Halloween Masks

When you live out in the country you experience Halloween differently than town kids do. The houses are far apart for trick or treat. Generally the people who live there do not have candy to give away.

One year our parents got together with the other neighbors and planned a little party for us. We liked that.

All of us bought a mask at the Five and Dime. They were fifteen cents each. They were made of gauze and covered with some kind of painted stuff. They always had a strange smell to them, especially when your mouth got the material wet. I loved the mask, but hated the smell.

We met at the McCall's home for the party. They lived about two miles from our house. They had a large cornfield behind their barn. The corn had been cut and tied into tall stacks in the rows.

We played indoor games, dunked for apples, popped balloons and got our masks even wetter.

Someone suggested that we play hide and seek out in the rows of corn stacks. It was quite dark, with only the moon giving a little light.

We chose one of the kids to find us. The rest headed out into the corn.

We were all hiding in the cornrows. All of a sudden, one of the girls screamed and started running fast towards the house. She was yelling,

"There is a strange man out there in the corn! He was standing right behind me!"

We all ran to the house. We were scared to death. The men grabbed a shotgun, flashlights and lanterns and headed towards the field. They shot the gun into the air. They found no one. If he was there, he was now gone.

On our walk home, Daddy said, "I think the girl just imagined that someone was there. That is the kind of thing that happens in cities. We don't have bad guys out here in the country."

We thought that he was trying to make Kenny and me feel safe and not to be scared to be out at night.

"The country is where good people live," he said. We hoped he was right.

MY ADVENTURES

There is a definite advantage to being raised in a poor family in a country setting.

With limited toys (or play-pretties, as we called them in the South), one has to improvise, substitute and many times invent things and games to make your life exciting.

Kenny and I did this as we moved through the first twelve years of our lives.

Our parents trusted us. We spent the summer days on our own in fields, woods and streams, without supervision. This freedom allowed us many of our adventures. Here are some of them.

The Train Scare

Kenny and I decided we would spend the summer day in town. We had nothing special planned. We just wanted to explore.

Somehow we found ourselves at the train yard watching the engines hooking and unhooking the freight cars. We got off our bikes and stood on a small train bridge with handrails on each side.

The bridge was about fifty feet long and went over a small creek. We walked to the middle of the bridge and held the handrail as the big engine and cars started coming toward us. The engineer was blowing his whistle and waving for us to get off the bridge. We could feel the suction from the train starting to pull us towards it. But it was too late to run off the bridge. The train was starting to move fast. We had no idea of the great amount of suction the train would create as it picked up speed. The sound was deafening.

I yelled to Kenny, " Hold on and pray." He started yelling, "Lord, don't let us get sucked under this train." We held on for dear life until the engine and eight freight cars were past.

I looked at Kenny. We were covered with soot. He finally started to smile. Boy was I glad to see those white teeth. I said, "You prayed good." He smiled again. Kenny believed in prayer more than I did and I believed in Kenny.

On the way home we stopped at a small creek, stripped off our clothes, waded in and tried to wash the soot from our faces. We did not want Momma and Daddy to know where the soot came from.

This had been a new adventure for us, one of many to come and one we would not forget anytime soon.

Smoking

One day I said to Kenny, "We should try smoking." He generally thought that my ideas were pretty good, so he said, "OK, but what are we going to smoke?" I said, "I have been thinking about it and I thought that we could take dried tree leaves, crush them up, roll them in newspaper and that should work."

We tried different kinds of leaves. Sweet Gum tree leaves seemed to work the best and tasted the best, too. We took an old newspaper, tore it into little squares of paper, and rolled ourselves some fine cigarettes.

Another day we were swinging on an old wild grape vine down in the woods. It had grown up into a tree. We used it as a swing. We were swinging on it and it broke. We were looking at the broken vine and discovered that the vine had a small hole that ran right through the center.

I said, "We will bring the hand saw down, cut the vine into pieces and we will have some long-lasting smokes."

We cut off three-inch pieces of the vine and lit them. They lasted most of the day. We sat in our thatched hut, smoked and wondered how many people in the world knew that wild grape vines had a hole down the middle. Probably not very many. We had made a very good discovery.

Playing with Gun Powder

Our neighbors up the Congo Road had a little money. They had a bathroom in their house. The father had a regular job and worked each day. The boy, Rex, was my age. He came into our yard one day and said, "I have made a new discovery–Come to my house and I will show you."

He had some 22-caliber bullets. He took two pairs of pliers and put one pair on the brass end of the bullet and the other pair on the lead part. He carefully pulled and twisted and the bullet came apart. There was gunpowder in the brass part. He emptied the gunpowder onto a short heavy piece of old railroad track and slammed it with a hammer. Man, did that make a loud bang!

After doing the gunpowder thing for about five days in a row, we were tiring of blasting the powder. We went back to playing marbles.

I Catch My Hand in the Washing Machine Wringer

Aunt Ola had a wringer washing machine on the back porch that had both hot and cold water. I was fascinated by it. I was lucky enough to sometimes be there on washday. She would fill the washer with hot boiling water, add some Duz soap powder and put in the clothes. She always washed the white clothes first, and then followed with the darks. I asked her why she washed the whites first. She did not have a good answer–that was just the way she did it.

She would turn it on and it would begin to buzz and soon the agitator would start to make a sound and we knew it was doing its job. She would check her watch and tell me that it should agitate for about an hour and then I could drain the water. I liked this part because we did not have running water at our house and I was fascinated by it.

Aunt Ola and I would go into the kitchen and get some graham crackers and a bottle of Dr. Pepper and sit and look through some of her magazines. She had *Life*, *Look*, *Collier's*, *Saturday Evening Post* and *Popular Mechanics* as well as several religious magazines and *Woman's Day* that had an article about the soap opera radio shows. She said that I could look at all of them except the one about soap operas. She said that it was for adults and sometimes it had articles about people being in love. She said I was too young to know about things like that.

So, I would look at all the others, and try to sneak a peek at the soap opera article when she went to the back porch to check on the wash. I would look fast, but could never figure out what I was not supposed to see. When she returned to the kitchen, I was always looking at the little ads in *Popular Mechanics*.

Soon she said that it was time to drain the water. I loved doing this part, so I jumped up and hurried to do the draining. Next we had to run the clothes that had been washed through the wringer in order to get all the soapy water out before we started to rinse them.

I wanted to do the wringing, so I jumped up on a stool next to the washer and started to feed the clothes into the wringer. Aunt Ola warned me to not get my fingers in the wringer. I told her I was always careful. I was trying to get a thick towel in the wringer, but was having trouble getting it to feed in. I pushed a little harder and I did not pull my hand back quickly enough. The wringer caught my fingers and started to pull my hand into it too. I screamed bloody murder for Aunt Ola to help me. She ran over and hit the release handle, but it wasn't turning off like it was supposed to do. She panicked, and then thought about unplugging the washer from the electricity. Uncle Judd was just coming into the house and heard all the yelling. He came running and saw the problem. My arm had gotten pulled in all the way up to my elbow. I was trying not to cry, but it was my right hand and arm that was in the wringer, the hand I did my drawing and painting with. What if I would never be able to draw and paint again!

Uncle Judd grabbed a large screwdriver and forced it between the wringer rollers until I could pull my arm out. I was hurting like the devil, but trying not to cry. Aunt Ola looked at it and said it was not smashed as bad as she had thought it would be. Uncle Judd agreed. I could wiggle all my fingers and turn my hand and move my elbow. But it had taken off some of my skin. Aunt Ola got out the bottle of peroxide and started to wash the wound until it was bubbling. She said to let it dry in the air and then she would bandage it. She put on some Mercurochrome and wrapped it.

I did not help Aunt Ola finish the wash. I was ready to go home. Uncle Judd said he would put my bike in the back of his pickup truck and carry me home.

When I got out of the truck, Momma saw me and asked what on earth I had done. I told her that I got caught in the wringer of the washer while I was helping Aunt Ola. Daddy came in and saw me and said he should give me a whipping for not being more careful. Momma told him that I had gone through enough pain and had learned my lesson.

I went to bed that night thinking that I had missed one of the parts of washing clothes that I really liked. It was when Aunt Ola would pour Mrs. Stewart's Bluing into the white clothes rinse water. Every time I would think the bluing was going to ruin the white clothes by making them blue, but it did not. It only made them look whiter. It was magic to me.

Stamp Approvals in the Mail

In a *Popular Mechanics* magazine, we found an ad that said that a stamp company would send us beautiful postage stamps on approval. We did not know what "on approval" meant. We did want to have stamps from many countries. We had started to collect stamps when I was nine years old and Kenny was six.

We sent an envelope, with another envelope inside with our address printed on it, just like it said to do. We also had to put a three-cent stamp on both the envelope we were sending and the return envelope. We had to pick up three extra cold drink bottles that day just to have the money to buy stamps.

For six cents worth of postage stamps, we were going to own many beautiful stamps.

We watched each day for the mailman's car to pull up to our mailbox. Finally he brought them.

We opened the envelope and inside were small clear envelopes with beautiful stamps. Some were even triangle shaped. They were all new, not even licked. We were ready to put them in our stamp book that recently had been given to us.

My Daddy said, "What are you two doing now?" We said, "A company that advertised in a magazine has sent free stamps to us as a gift." Daddy read the letter. He said, "You have to pay for these." We thought he was teasing us. "No," he said, "Approval means you can look at them and if you like them, then you approve, and keep the stamps and send the company money."

This would mean we had to pick up many bottles to pay for them. So we picked up two bottles and bought a three-cent stamp and still had a penny to buy a piece of bubble gum. We split the bubble gum equally and returned the stamps. We did not approve.

Free Stuff

We did not get a lot of toys. Our folks simply did not have the money. We did find that there were free gifts in some things that you buy.

One day my Momma bought a box of Shredded Wheat cereal, which had three layers of shredded biscuits in the box. Between each layer was a piece of cardboard. On each piece they had printed small houses that you cut out, fold, and glue the tabs to make little three-dimensional houses. These were great. I ate the cereal fast so Momma would buy another box.

My Uncle Judd sometimes would buy Kenny and me boxes of Cracker Jacks. They always had great little toys in the boxes. Uncle Judd was rich. He had an indoor bathroom with running water. He could buy all the candy he wanted. He never did buy Cracker Jacks for himself. He liked peanut candy, especially peanut brittle.

One day when we were in Mr. Stuart's grocery store, the little grocery that would let Momma charge things, Kenny and I spied a Wheaties cereal box that had miniature car license tags glued to the outside of the box. The tag was made out of metal, just like the real car tags. Each box on the shelf had a different state tag.

Man, oh man, we liked this new idea. We immediately did not like Shredded Wheat any more. We wanted Wheaties because it is "the breakfast of champions" and it has miniature car tags.

We were always sure to be with Momma when she went to Mr. Stuart's store so we could pick out the state tag we wanted. We had collected several state tags each. Kenny's Momma also bought him Wheaties.

Another day we went into the store to see if there was a box with a New Mexico tag on it. To our surprise, the box had words that said, "Collectors State Car Tags Now Inside Box." This was not good because it did not tell which state tag was inside the box.

We asked Mr. Suart why the company had done this. He said, "Because in the wicked big cities kids were stealing them by tearing off the car tags from the box and not buying the cereal."

We were very upset. This was terrible. Momma could not afford to buy boxes of Wheaties only to find a car tag inside that we already had.

We thought the city kids that did this should be ashamed for having ruined a good thing.

We went back to eating Shredded Wheat. Then we could have more cardboard houses to color.

New Bow and Arrows

One summer the people in our church collected money to send me to camp.

I loved camp. We went swimming every day in a beautiful lake, played baseball, had campfires and did craft projects, too.

One craft they offered was making real bows, the kind that shoots arrows. I chose this as my craft. They gave each of us a rough ash bow that was already cut. We had to sand and finish it. The bows were free. We did not have to pay for them. I could not believe it.

I sanded the bow until it had a really fine finish. I was so proud. We put real bowstrings on the bows. The camp teacher also gave each one of us two arrows. Free.

In the afternoon they taught us how to shoot them. We shot the arrows into bales of hay.

When I returned home I could not wait to have all the neighbor kids over to see my new bow.

We nailed an old board to a tree as our target. We shot arrows at the board for a while. I let each kid take a turn. Kenny thought he should get two turns, so I let him.

After the other kids went home, I told Kenny, "Let's shoot an arrow straight up into the air. We will keep our eye on it until it reaches its peak, then it will turn and start coming straight down. We have to watch carefully so we don't get hurt. We can make a game of it. We will draw a circle on the ground, stand in the circle, and watch as the arrow starts coming down at full speed. The first one to run from the circle is a sissy."

Kenny looked at me for a long time. Finally, he said, "You think we won't get hurt?"

I said, "Not if we watch carefully, but remember, don't be a sissy." This was our first experience with this new game. I would shoot the arrow straight up and watch it reach its peak. Then we would watch as it came streaking to the ground. I would yell. "RUN" at the last moment and we would scatter.

We did this a number of times. An arrow never hit either of us, but there were many close calls.

One day, Daddy came home and saw what we were doing. He got pretty mad and threatened to burn my bow. We both promised we would not do that anymore.

Generally, during the daytime, we were home alone all summer. It sure slowed down our fun when the adults were around.

Feeding the Fish

Kenny and I loved to swim in the rivers close to our home. In the Saline River there is a swimming hole we call Jones' Landing, because the Jones' General Store is right by the swimming place. It was our favorite. We bought candy and cold drinks there, too.

We each saved our money to buy a swim mask to wear under water.

When we were swimming at Jones' we always felt small fish trying to nibble our legs. We thought it would be neat to be able to go under water and see just what kind of fish it was that was pestering us.

We bought our swim masks and headed for the river. We did not even stop at Jones' store for a cold drink. We waded into the river, held our breath, went under water and stayed very still. Little perch started swimming to our legs. They were about four-five inches long. We thought they were cute.

When we came up from the water, I said to Kenny, " It would be great if we could feed them." We came up with a great idea. "The next time we come swimming, we will bring some earthworms with us." We wanted to see if the fish would eat them out of our hands.

A week later, we dug some worms and rode our bikes to the river. We each put a few worms into the pockets of our swim trunks and waded into the water. We put on our swim masks and slowly went below the surface. We each held a worm in our hand. Immediately the little fish swam up to the worms and started to eat them. We watched in amazement. We had them eating out of our hands!

We came up for air, and I said to Kenny, "The city kids have aquariums and they have to reach over the glass walls of their tanks to feed their fish. We have our own 'aquarium' that we actually get into with the fish to feed them. The city kids don't have anything on us."

We fed the fish until the worms were gone. We went home happy.

Kenny Falls in the New-dug Well

Kenny and I were always thinking of new games to play. One day I suggested that we circle round the new well being dug and see who could get closest to the edge without falling in. Kenny liked the idea.

Kenny's Momma was having a new well dug by an older teenage boy who lived next door. His name was Coy and he was very strong.

There had been rain. Coy had not been digging for a few days. There was no fence around the well. It was still a bit muddy, but we thought that would make it more adventuresome.

Coy had dug down about ten feet before it started raining and he had to stop.

We started to circle the well, about a foot away from the edge at first, then six inches, then right up to the edge. Kenny slipped. Kenny fell into the well.

There was about a foot of water in the well. It helped cushion his fall a bit. He went in feet first.

Kenny started yelling at the top of his voice, "Help! Get me out of this well! I am sure there are snakes in this water!"

I lay on my belly, slid over to the edge and looked down. Kenny had water all over him. He was trying to climb up the steep walls of the well.

I said, "Are you hurt bad? Did you break you leg or foot?" He said, "I don't think so, but I am going to die from snake bites. Get me out of here!" I said, "I don't see any snakes." He said, "That's because they stay under water until they bite you and then you die! I don't want to die in a well! Get help!"

I ran to Coy's house. No one was home. I ran over the hill to Fricky Johnson's house. I yelled, "Mrs. Johnson, Kenny fell in the well and I need your help." She looked at me and said, "Are you teasing me?" I said, "No ma'am, Kenny is in the well at his house!"

Johnny came around the house and Fricky yelled for him to get two ropes. We all started to run up the hill as fast as we could.

When we got near the well, we could hear Kenny yelling out a prayer, "Lord, save me from these wicked snakes in this well!" I think he thought he needed to yell because he was so far down in the well that the Lord might not be able to hear him.

We all ran to the well and lay on our stomachs and tried to reassure Kenny that we were going to save him. He was starting to cry.

Fricky made a loop in the rope and tied a knot in it so Kenny could put his foot in the loop. She dropped the rope down in the well and said, "Boy, you stop that crying and listen to me". She told him to put one of his feet into the loop and hold onto the rope. We would pull him out.

Kenny did as he was told. We all started to pull together on the rope. The problem was that the clay was slick from the rain and we all started to slide towards the edge. Fricky yelled, "Stop!" Kenny was about two feet above the water. He started yelling, "Don't stop now! There are snakes down here!"

Fricky looked at us out of one crossed eye, and then the other. "Shit!" That's all she said. Then she thought for a minute and yelled to me, "Tie one rope around that small tree over yonder and tie the other end of it around me." She and Johnny were trying to keep Kenny above the water without sliding in.

I hurried and did as I was told. Now Fricky would not slide in. She told Johnny and me, "Get hold of the rope between me and the tree and every time I yell PULL! you pull for all you are worth." We pulled Fricky and she pulled Kenny.

Kenny was whimpering. He was only seven years old, so I thought it was OK to whimper. We all pulled and pulled. We finally saw the top of his head, then his eyes. They looked mad and scared. We kept on pulling until we finally had him up on the ground. We all looked like a mess with mud all over us.

I asked Kenny, "Did any snakes bite you?" He said, "No, but I know they were trying to figure how they could eat me alive."

Fricky sat there. Then she asked the question I knew was coming: "Child, what on earth were you doing near that well without a fence around it?" I tried to come up with a good answer that would save us from looking stupid. Would Fricky believe it if I told her we were chasing a ball and didn't see the well, or perhaps, we lost our cat and wanted to see if it had fallen in the well and Kenny slipped in?

No, I knew we had to tell the truth, so I told her that we were playing a game and I won. I did not fall in the well.

We thanked Fricky and Johnny. She told Johnny, "You come home with me, where it is safe." Then she looked at Kenny and me out of one eye and then the other. She did not say goodbye.

I Hit Kenny in the Head

The new refrigerator came in a plywood box. Daddy and I unpacked it and slid the refrigerator out. I asked Daddy if Kenny and I could use it to build a clubhouse. He said yes, and we were so happy.

We laid it on its side with the end of it open. It was perfect.

One day we were playing in it and I was nailing some boards around the top of the opening in order to make a door. I was nailing away when Kenny crawled out from inside the clubhouse, right below where I was hammering. He caught my eye just as I was bringing down the hammer to hit the nail. By looking away for a moment, I missed the nail and hit Kenny right in the front of his head. He fell back into the clubhouse and just lay there. Blood was spurting out of his head.

In a few seconds he opened his eyes, grabbed his head and said, "What happened?"

Then he saw the blood on his hand and looked at me with fear in his eyes. There was no one at home. We were alone. I ran to the kitchen and grabbed a towel and came back and told Kenny we had to get help. He asked if he was going to die. I said, "No, you are going to live." He started praying, "Lord, don't let me die." I told him I had to get him down to Fricky's house so she could help us. I had to take him on my bike.

I told him to hold the towel tight against his head. I put him on the carriage rack behind the seat of my bike, and peddled as fast as I could. I kept asking, "Are you all right, Kenny?" and he would only say, "Yeah."

We rode into Fricky's yard and I started yelling for her to come and help. She and Johnny came out of the house and she said, "Oh Lord, what have you boys done now?" She picked Kenny up and carried him to the porch. She told Johnny to draw some fresh water from the well and for him to hurry. She got a clean cloth and started to try to clean the wound. It was still spurting blood. I was scared to death.

Then Fricky used her miracle cure. She put her finger in her mouth, dug out a wad of snuff from her lower lip and applied it to Kenny's head. She held the cloth tight against his head for a few minutes. She took away the cloth and it was still spurting a little. She dug out more snuff and applied it. In a few minutes, it had stopped spurting. She wound a cloth around his head.

She said for us to stay a while to make sure Kenny did not go to sleep. I asked Fricky why she did not put new dry snuff right out of the snuff can on the wound. She said that the used snuff from her lip worked better, as though it had some magic in it. She also said that using new snuff would just be wasting good snuff when she could use it first.

After about half an hour Fricky thought it was all right for me to take Kenny back home. I put him on the bike and pushed him and the bike up the hill towards home. I was not thrilled to think about what my Momma and Kenny's Momma were going to say when they got home from work and saw Kenny's head wrapped in a cloth bandage, like the picture I saw at school of the painter Van Gogh, after he had cut off his ear.

I thought I might be in a little trouble. But accidents do happen.

Don't Get Run Over by a Dead Chicken

Momma made fried chicken dinners for special occasions, like Easter and Christmas, and sometimes for my birthday. Today is my birthday.

We raised a few chickens in order to have eggs to eat. When Momma was going to have fried chicken, she had to kill one of them. This was a day that was both frightening and exciting for me. I told Kenny he had to see this. This would be a new experience for him.

Momma got the axe out of the barn and started trying to catch one of the chickens. Kenny and I tried to help her. We finally caught one. She took the chicken over to a stump in the yard and put its neck on the stump. I told Kenny not to watch. I watched. I was a big boy. I had just turned ten years old today.

She brought down the axe and the body of the chicken dropped to the ground and it started to run. It was amazing. The head was lying on the stump, but the chicken's body did not know it. For a few seconds it started to run in wild circles around the yard. Kenny and I ran to keep out of its way. We did not want to have blood all over us. Kenny was yelling, "Don't let the chicken attack me." So I yelled, "Then run faster."

We were amazed that something without a head could still move so swiftly. Maybe chickens have their brains in some other part of the body than the head.

Finally, the chicken body fell over and just lay there. We stopped running.

Momma had a pot of water boiling in a big black kettle over an outdoor fire pit. She dunked the chicken in the hot water. She did this to make the feathers come out easier. Feathers dunked in boiling water did not smell good. But we knew the chicken would be delicious when Momma got it fried.

Later that day, she put a special meal on the table. We had Kenny, his Momma and Aunt Ola and Uncle Judd over. Momma had also made her wonderful dinner rolls. She put a big platter of fried chicken, mashed potatoes, white gravy, boiled greens, fried okra and a salad in front of us. It looked delicious. She then put my favorite cake on the table. It was a pineapple upside-down cake with ten candles on it. We would light them later, after we finished our meal.

Kenny spied the chicken. He got a funny look on his face. His eyes got big. He suddenly realized that we were about to eat the same chicken that was spurting blood and chasing us all around the yard. I knew what was coming. He was going to tell the whole exciting gruesome story to everyone.

Before he could say anything, I said, "Kenny, tell us the story about when you fell in the well." He did not want to tell that one. He wanted to tell about the chicken killing, which was the first one he had ever seen. Momma realized what is happening too. She quickly said, "Let us thank the Lord for the food he has given us."

As she was ready to say the prayer, Kenny said, "Granny, don't forget to pray for the poor chicken we had to kill, because I don't think the chicken will be so happy with the Lord for having given her to us for our dinner."

Daddy laughed at Kenny's request.

Momma prayed, then she passed the chicken around the table. When it came to Kenny, he said, "I don't think I would like chicken today, but I will have some mashed potatoes and gravy."

Kenny hesitated for a minute and said, "Granny, if I don't eat the chicken, can I still have some of Clyde's delicious birthday cake?"

Momma said, "Yes." She understood.

The Carnival is Back in Town

Every spring the carnival returned to our little town in Arkansas. The carnival announced its arrival by moving arc lights slowly across the night sky. It was 1953 and I was twelve years old. I had been waiting with great excitement for the carnival to arrive. I had been saving money so I could go and try to win a teddy bear or something they say you can win.

One Saturday night, Momma, Daddy and I watched the bright beams from the arc spotlights crisscrossing the sky above our house. I asked, "Can I go to the carnival tomorrow?" They said, "It will be OK as long as you are careful and don't let the carnival people kidnap you and take you with them when they leave town." I laughed and said, " I don't have any act that they could use in the side shows."

The next day I rode my bike, alone, to the carnival grounds. I decided not to ask my best friend Kenny to go with me. I thought he was too young to see some of the things they might have there.

As I arrived, I found a barbed wire fence surrounding the carnival grounds. Everyone needed to pass through the entrance gate. You had to pay ten cents to enter.

After entering the grounds, I saw a banner on a tent that said, "*Throw Balls and Win Every time.*" I paid the man ten cents. He handed me four balls and said, "You have to knock over all four bottles to win the Teddy Bear." I wanted to win the Teddy Bear for my Momma. The bottles were spread out on the shelf, which made it difficult to knock all of them over.

I threw the balls and knocked over three of the four bottles. I asked the man what I had won. He gave me a little plastic pin that said, "I WON!" That lousy plastic pin cost me ten cents.

I played a number of other carnival games, but somehow the carnival people always manage to beat you. I bought fried dough, a snow cone and cotton candy until my money was almost gone.

I saw a tent with a large painting showing *The Two-Headed Man*, *The Fat Lady*, *The Man Covered With Fish Scales*, and *The Twin Siamese Midgets*. The ticket cost twenty-five cents to enter.

I had one quarter left. I paid the man the quarter. He asked me, "Are you old enough to see what they are going to show in there?" I said, "Yes'ir, I think so." He me let enter.

Inside, I could not believe the way they had tricked us about the *Two-Headed Man*. The "second head" was actually a large growth on his neck. They announced that it was another head that he was growing. Next came the *Man with Fish Scales*. I think they were real. I thought his Momma swam in the river too near the fish before he was born. Then I saw the *Twin Siamese Midgets*. I was very concerned about them having to do everything together, but I loved them. They were little and cute and I thought they would be fun playmates for Kenny.

For the last act, the drum rolled and the *Fat Lady* came upon the stage. Man, was she fat! She strutted around a bit then she started to do something strange. She took off her robe and there were two huge naked bosoms starring out at me! Each one had a tassel thing attached.

She started swinging one bosom to the right and the other to the left! They were going round and round, one clockwise, and the other counter-clockwise.

I was getting dizzy just trying to keep up with them. I knew my Momma would not want me seeing this. But Momma was not here so I kept watching.

Then *The Fat Lady* spied me in the crowd and said, "Boy, aren't you too young to be in here?" I did not know what to say. There are times when a young boy loses his voice. Finally, I said, "Yes, Ma'am, I might be." She teased, "Do you want to come up here on the stage and see my 'mountains and the valley between them', up real close?" I had already had been too close to my Aunt Madeline's "*mountains*" when she hugged me real tight the last time she visited us, and I did not like the smell of her mountains. This fat lady's "*mountains*" made Aunt Madeline's bosoms look like small hills. I was not going to get close enough to smell *The Fat Lady's* "*mountains,* or her "*valley.*"

I jumped out of my seat and ran fast out of the tent. Everyone laughed. I did not. I was glad Kenny was not here to experience this, with him being only nine years old. He was just a bit too young.

After I caught my breath I saw another sideshow in a house-like trailer. It had a door at each end. The sign said "*Free, See the Man in the Iron Lung*" At school, I had heard about people who had polio having to live in Iron Lungs in order to breathe. I thought, this show is free, it will be educational and I am out of money, so this will be perfect.

I entered where the sign said, "*Enter Here.*" There were a lot of people waiting to get into this free event. I waited in line. Soon I was looking through a glass panel placed in the side of the Iron Lung. I could see the man's chest going up and down as the iron lung made him breathe. I felt a bit embarrassed as I smiled at the man lying there.

After watching the huge iron lung help the man breathe, I decided to go back outside.

As I started to leave, there was a real giant of a man at the exit door. He held out his hand and said, *"Ten cents, please."* I was shocked and said, "The sign said *Free Entry."*

He said, "It is free to get in, but you have to give a silver donation to *get out*. That means a dime or a quarter, as both are made of silver." I said, "But I don't have any money!" Frowning, he stared at me and said, "So you want to be the next person to lay in the Iron Lung?"

That scared me to death. I made a run for the door. He was yelling for me to stop, but I was moving out, trying to find my bicycle. I jumped on it and peddled home as fast as I could.

I had enough of the carnival for one day, having had my first "real mountain" experience, and almost having to lay in The Iron Lung.

When I got home, Momma and Daddy asked me if I had an exciting day at the carnival. I said, "Yeah, I tried to win you a teddy bear, Momma, but it didn't work. I bought some good things to eat and I played a few games. I also saw a freak show as well as some nice mountains.

They did not ask anything more and I was relieved. I just don't think they would like the fact that I had just seen some of those "evil sinful things" the preacher spoke about in his sermon just last week.

I was tired. I went to bed, thinking, "I don't think Momma and Daddy need to worry about me running off with the carnival people."

Grass for Snacks

Kenny and I liked to experiment with wild growing things that we could eat. We ate many types of wild berries, plums, green apples and several types of wild grass. We were not sure if some of the things we ate were poisonous or not. I told Kenny to try them first, since he was younger. He should eat them, and then, if he got sick, I would know how to go for help, because I was older. He was not wild about this idea but he went along with it.

We discovered a light green grass with little yellow flowers that looked like a small shamrock. It had a very sour taste when you ate it. The yellow flowers tasted sour too. We loved them.

We found a grey grass plant that had a black pepper taste. It was kind of spicy and hot, too. It was also a favorite. We called it "pepper grass." We had no idea what the real names of the grasses were.

After our morning snack of grasses and berries, we went into the house and I fixed dinner. I opened the peanut butter jar and put some in a bowl. I poured dark Karo Corn Syrup in and mixed it. We liked to spread the concoction on White Wonder Bread because it *"Builds Strong Bodies Eight Ways."* Even though we didn't know what the eight ways were, we believed the commercials we heard on the radio. A big company like Wonder Bread would not lie to kids.

Both the wild things and the peanut butter-syrup sandwiches were really good. We preferred the sandwiches, though. They were more filling.

Sheep in the Sky

March and April in Arkansas were still cool and the winds began to blow. Kenny and I liked to lie in the tall grass in the field behind our house and watch the clouds as the wind blew over us. The tall grass protected us from the wind. We were warm lying there.

We watched all kinds of imaginary animals and things in the clouds. They were always changing. We watched a herd of clouds turn into a herd of sheep. We watched dogs turn into elephants and giraffes turn into kittens.

One day I said to Kenny, "Look, there is a naked woman in the clouds." He looked and said, "I don't see no naked woman. Where is she?" I told him, "Look harder before she changes into a flower or something. Look fast!" He said he could not see it. He was getting mad.

Of course I was only teasing him but he did not know it. I told him, "You missed your chance and it may be years before you get to see another naked woman."

Kenny was only seven years old. I should not have teased him like that.

We Find an Old Moonshine Still

Kenny and I thought we knew every square foot of land within five miles of our house. One day we made a brand-new discovery.

We were hiking into an area that we had been many times before. We happened upon a rabbit in the field. We started chasing the rabbit. All of a sudden, the rabbit disappeared under some heavy brush and went out of sight. We started looking more closely and discovered that there was a big gully totally covered with brush and pine trees. They were growing out of the sunken area. The trees had very low hanging limbs that covered the ground, hiding it from view. We had walked by this spot many times and were not aware that this hidden place even existed.

We got down on our hands and knees and started to crawl into the unknown. It opened up into a large room with only tree branches for a ceiling. It was quite dark and our eyes had to adjust. To our utter amazement, we started to see various metal pipes that wrapped around in circles, a large copper tank and an old copper tub. There was a fire pit made of rocks and also a spring, bubbling pure clear water. Someone had taken an old oak barrel and sunk into the ground creating a wonderful spring.

We realized that we had discovered an old whisky still from years ago, hidden away, even from us. I told Kenny, "We have found an old still that is probably from the 1930s. This copper is worth a lot of money!" We both just stood there in amazement. We had never heard anyone speak of an old still around these parts. I said, "Should we tell anyone or should we just keep our secret from everyone, and I mean everyone…even Johnny Johnson?"

Kenny said, "Clyde, this is a beautiful place that no one knows about. If someone had known about it, they would have taken the copper pipes and tub and tank and sold it long ago. I think it should be our secret and only we will get to come here when we want to and enjoy it. It will just be ours."

After our discovery, we continued to visit our secret hiding place every summer. We would pack peanut butter and Karo Syrup sandwiches, a jar of Kool Aid and slip away and just lie on the ground floor in the cool space of our new hideaway, light up and smoke our grapevine smokes and listen to the wind blowing through the pine branches above us. We had our own paradise that not even the government men knew about.

We swore to never tell anyone and we didn't.

The Stuck Lollypop

One day I was home alone. I was nine years old, sucking on a red Safety Pop sucker. It was the type that had a twisted paper string handle that made a loop.

I sucked on it for a while. Then I started to bite it hard and chew it into smaller pieces in order to swallow it. But, before I had a chance to chew it into small pieces, somehow a large piece went down my throat. It hung there. Stuck. I could still breathe as it was stuck standing up in my throat. But the pain was awful. It would not go down.

I panicked. What could I do? The thought hit me that I needed warm water to dissolve it. But we did not have running water and certainly not hot water. I grabbed the teakettle, poured in some water from the bucket and put it on the stove to heat it. I was in pain. It seemed forever, but the water got warm and I poured some into a cup and drank it slowly.

Finally the large piece of hard candy dissolved enough for me to swallow. I made up my mind that I had it with Safety Pop suckers. From now on, I would stick to the caramel all-day Slow Poke suckers.

Johnny's Red Hair

Besides Kenny, my best friend was Johnny Johnson who lived down Shady Grove Road. Kenny and I played a lot down at his house during the summers. Johnny's house was near Mr. Gerard's pond. We skinny-dipped in the pond and fished there with our cane poles and worms.

One day while we were with Johnny, he said, "I hate my red hair." He really did have red hair. I said, "We should get on our bikes and go buy a bottle of black hair dye and we will help you get rid of your red hair."

He sort of liked the idea. Two hours later we three had picked up enough cold drink bottles along the highway to buy the dye. After selling the bottles to Mr. Lacky's, we rode into town to Mr. Gingle's Drug store.

We looked at the colors of hair dye and chose one that was Jet Black. "This should do the trick," Kenny said. After paying for the dye we had twenty cents left. We all bought a nickel ice cream cone and five pieces of bubble gum. This meant two pieces of bubble gum for two of us and one for the other.

The man behind the counter saw our situation. He leaned over the counter and gave us one more piece for free. We thanked him and jumped on our bikes and headed back to Gerard's pond.

We all stripped off our clothes and waded into the pond with the bottle of Jet Black Hair Dye. I read the label. It said, "*wet the hair and then apply the dye and wait a few minutes before rinsing it out.*"

Johnny dunked his head under the water. I started to pour the black dye on his head and started to rub it in with my hands. We were not sure what the label meant about applying the dye, but it seemed to be working.

After a few minutes, I said, "Johnny, dunk your head under water again to rinse it." When he did all the water around us started turning black. We all thought that it was going to make our skin black, but it did not. If it had made our skin black, I think my Daddy would have beat the tar out of me because he could not have a son with black skin.

When Johnny came up after dunking his head the second time we started to laugh. He looked completely different, like someone we didn't know. He asked, "How do I look?" We said, "Great."

After we air-dried our naked bodies in the sun, we put on our clothes and headed back to Johnny's' house. His mother Fricky, who was very cross-eyed, looked at us coming through the gate into the yard. She was staring and said, "Clydie, is that you and Kenny?" We said, "Yes, ma'am." She asked, "Who is that with you?" She did not realize it was her own son Johnny.

She looked at him with one eye and then the other. I said, "It is Johnny, Mrs. Johnson." She spit her snuff juice on the ground and she started getting fiery mad. She started coming at Johnny. Kenny and I jumped on our bikes and headed for home.

We looked back and saw her grabbing Johnny by the hair. We did not wait to see what else happened.

Johnny lived through his Momma's anger, but he sure looked funny when his hair started growing and half of it was red and half was black.

Flying Kites

When the March winds came, Kenny and I would build kites.

There were tall weeds that grew down behind the house. The weeds died in winter. They were hollow and had a hole down the center of them. They were very lightweight after drying during the winter months. They were as long as six feet and made great sticks for our kites.

We would tie the sticks together with string to make the shape of the kite, then run a string around the outside of the shape.

We cut newspaper to size, then glued the paper to the string with flour paste that we made. It was just white baking flour and water. The store-bought mucilage could only be used for school projects, as it was too expensive to use for things like kite building. Our flour paste worked just fine. We cut up old pieces of cloth and tied them together to make the tail. The only thing we had to get from a store was the kite string.

We spent whole days flying our kites, as long as the wind continued to blow.

One time a friend of my older brother brought a real kite to us from the Five and Dime. It was a beautiful light blue color and had real kite sticks. It was wonderful because it was lightweight. It made a rattling sound when the wind was blowing against the thin blue tissue paper. We had seen kites like this at the Five and Dime and they cost fifteen cents each. We were so impressed.

We were flying our magnificent rattling blue kite one day when the string broke. The kite floated down into the field across the road from our house, right into the field where Mr. Carver had his two prize Brahma Bulls. It landed right between the bulls. The bulls looked at the kites, then at us. My Daddy told us never to go into the field with them, because they were dangerous.

I told Kenny that we had to somehow get to our kite before the bulls tromped on it. I said, "Let's make a plan. We will crawl through the barbed wire fence, then I will stay near the fence and jump up and down and holler. I will try to get the bulls attention." All Kenny had to do was sneak over and try to get the kite while I jumped up and down and hollered, staying near the fence for my escape. Kenny looked at me like I was stupid or something.

He said, "I will do the jumping and hollering and you do the sneaking."

I told him, "You are smaller and the bulls will not notice you sneaking, but they will notice me."

Just then Mr. Carver must have seen us and recognized our predicament. He took a metal grain bucket and started hitting it with a stick and started calling the bulls to come and get the feed.

The bulls looked at Mr. Carver, then they looked at the kite and then at us. I said to Kenny, "Pray that the Lord will make them hungry for the grain and not for us." Kenny prayed. It worked.

One of the bulls went over to the kite and put his hoof almost over it, but then Mr. Carver hit the bucket again and the bulls turned and slowly walked towards him.

We got our kite and the next day we added more string to our spool to fly it higher towards the heavens. We cut a small square of paper and wrote *Thank you Jesus*. We placed the string through the hole in the paper and let it go. The wind currents slowly carried the note up the string until it reached the kite. This was as high as we could get it towards heaven.

Jesus would have to do the rest.

King's Silverware

Some of our favorite wild snacks were things we found on trees. We ate muscadines, which were like a grape with thick skin and seeds. We also ate red and yellow wild plums. It seemed that they all had a tiny worm in each one, but Daddy said, "Just think of the worms as protein." This sounded OK to us. The yellow plums were the sweetest, just like the yellow watermelons we raised were sweeter than the red ones.

One day while we were eating wild persimmons from a very old persimmon tree, one of us bit the long slim seed in half the long way. We were so surprised when we looked inside and saw a perfect shape of a fork, the kind you eat with. We wondered if we bit another in half if it would have a fork in it too. To our surprise, it had a perfect knife like you use to butter your biscuit. Now we were getting excited. We bit into another and found a spoon, then another knife and another fork.

I said, "We should call it the King's Silverware." We did, and we kept our secret for a long time because we did not think people would believe us. One day we told Daddy about finding something special at the old persimmon tree up by Shady Grove Road. He said, "Did you find the old black snake that lives in the base of the tree?"

After that we decided that some things should be kept secret from adults. We were not going to share the King's silverware with anyone else. We never did see the old black snake. I thought Daddy was teasing us.

After that, we always used the snake stick to poke around the tree before sitting under it to eat persimmons.

Crystal Radio

I read about how to make a crystal radio that did not need batteries or electricity to make it play. I found a crystal advertised in a magazine for twenty-five cents. You also had to order an earphone piece in order to hear the radio play. The earphone cost one dollar.

I waited for the mailman in his ugly Nash car to top the hill on Congo Road. He stopped at our mailbox and asked, "What are you ordering this time and is this a moneymaking deal?" I told him, "No, this is for a kit to make a crystal radio and that it is just for my own entertainment. No one can hear, except the one with the earphone."

A week later the mailman brought it to me.

The crystal was a small piece of something that looked like soft metal and about the size of a dime. It came with a little roll of copper wire. The directions said, "Wind the wire around and around a small board. Then cut a tin can into a small strip and nail the strip to be the board. This will to be used as the tuner."

I hooked it up and moved the tuner tin piece across the wound wires and, low and behold, I could hear our local small-town radio station. The only problem was that the small radio stations were required to go off the air at sunset. I guess it was some dumb government rule. So, at night, I would carefully move the tuner and could sometimes pick up the stronger Little Rock station twenty five miles away.

Then I could hear country music and baseball games until I went to sleep.

There were times though when I would take the wire off the crystal and just listen for the train winding through the valley and the trucks on the highway in the distance. The most exciting night sound was hearing the Ashby Funeral Home ambulance wailing towards Little Rock and the hospital.

I always wondered what had happened and who was in the ambulance. Hopefully no one I knew.

Playing Under the Sweet Gum Tree

Johnny Johnson, Kenny and I loved to play in the sandy dirt in front of our house. Kenny and I had a few "Dinky" metal cars and trucks. Johnny did not have any little toys.

When we played in the dirt at his house, we would push small glass jars and bottles around. We made believe they were trucks and cars.

We played around the roots of the large sweet gum tree in our yard. It was fun to make tunnels under the roots. We made make-believe houses out of small blocks of wood. We dug holes and put small cans in the holes, filled them with water and had lakes.

One day while we were playing, Johnny said that he liked to come to my house to play with our toys. Kenny and I looked at each other. We did not need to say a word. I said, "Johnny, Kenny and I would like you to have a car or truck. Pick out any two you want." He got a big grin on his face–then, it changed. He said, "My Daddy told me not to accept gifts from other people." We said he means *other people*, he does not mean *us*. Johnny said, "Yes, I think he means anybody."

We thought for a few minutes about what he had said. I said, "We can all three go along the road and pick up cold drink bottles and sell them to Mr. Lacky. Then you will have money and you can buy them from us." Kenny smiled, Johnny grinned.

In about two hours, we had picked up enough bottles to cash in for fifty cents. We said, "Each of our cars are worth twenty-five cents." He gave us the fifty cents. He was really grinning now. He chose a red truck from me, and a blue car from Kenny.

He told us goodbye and went running down the road to his house, the proud owner of two little cars.

Making Coins Bright and Shiny

Ralph brought something to school that was new to us. It was mercury, the silver liquid that is in thermometers. He said he broke some old thermometers to get the liquid. He had it in a small bottle. He said it was like magic.

He poured a bit onto a table and it broke into a lot of small balls. They were all bright and shiny. He pushed all the little balls together and they became a larger ball again. We watched and said, "Magic!" He said, "There's more–wait and see."

He took a dime out of his pocket and picked up a small amount of the Mercury with his fingers. He rubbed both sides of the dime. Boy, did he make it shine. "Special, spectacular, magic!" we said. He said that you could do the same to a quarter, or half dollar as they were made of silver. Nobody had a quarter or a half dollar piece.

After school, Kenny and I picked up cold drink bottles along the road and sold them to Mr. Lacky. We each had a dime to take to school the next day.

We took our dimes in our pockets. Ralph gave us a little of his mercury. We put it between our fingers and rubbed it on our dimes. It made them beautiful and shiny. We put them back in our pockets. We were going to keep these. We would not use them to buy candy or cold drinks. These were very special.

Own a One-inch Square of Land in the Yukon

Kenny and I liked to listen to the radio show, *Sergeant Preston of the Yukon*. The program was about Sergeant Preston of the Northwest Territory Royal Mounted Police. He had a great Husky dog, named Yukon King. The Sergeant and his Husky fought the evil men in the Northwestern Canadian wilderness.

We loved the show and listened on Tuesdays and Thursdays each week. The Quaker Oats Company sponsored the program. The Company was always trying to get kids to have their mommas buy Puffed Rice or Puffed Wheat.

We asked Momma to buy a box of Puffed Rice. Kenny and I tried it, but did not like it too much. We ate all of the Puffed Rice, and then went back to eating Wheaties.

One day while we were listening to Sergeant Preston, the radio announcer said, "Today Quaker Oats wants to give kids a free gift. When you buy a box of Quaker Puffed Rice or Puffed Wheat, we will give you one square inch of land where Sergeant Preston and Yukon King live." He went on to say, "All you have to do is buy a box of either Puffed Rice or Puffed Wheat, remove the box top and send it to Quaker Oats to receive your certificate of ownership of land where Sergeant Preston lives in the Yukon. The more Puffs you buy, the more land you own. So, get Mom to purchase Puffs today and send in the box top to own free land. And now, back to Sergeant Preston and Yukon King"

Kenny and I looked at each other. I said, "We could own a square inch of land where Sergeant Preston lives. For free! If we buy more Puffs, we can own more land." This was terrific. We asked our mommas to please buy Quaker Puffs, either Puffed Wheat or Puffed Rice. We did not really like Puffs that much, so we did not care which they bought. We knew we would have to eat them though.

We listened, we bought, and we ate. We cut the box tops and sent them to Quaker Oats over the next couple of months until the company announced that the "Free Land Giveaway" was over.

We now each owned several square inches of land in the Yukon. We knew there had to be oil or gold under our piece of land. "When we are grown, we will have to cash in on the profits," Kenny said.

We switched back to cereals that we liked better than Puffed Rice or Wheat.

The Quaker Oats people would have to come up with another great plan to win us back, but we continued to listen to *Sergeant Preston of the Yukon and his faithful dog, Yukon King.*

Someday we would be rich from our land purchase, thanks to Sergeant Preston and Quaker Oats.

The New Drive-in Theater

A new Drive-in Theater had been built on the highway between Benton and Little Rock, only about a mile from our house. They had metal lawn chairs set up outside the concessions booth, so people could get out of their hot cars in the summer and watch the movie in the breeze, if there was any.

Kenny and I rode our bikes into the drive-in grounds one day when they were closed. We discovered the metal chairs and I said, "If we can sneak into the drive-in from the back, we can sit in the chairs and watch a free movie."

We told Johnny Johnson about our idea. He liked it. We knew our Mommas would not like it. Momma and Fricky did not think we should go to those evil movies. They thought it was the Devil's playground. We finally talked them into letting us go. We told them it was free if you did not have a car.

We started going once a week. We would hide our bikes out back, and then sneak into the movie grounds. We would sit in the metal chairs and act like we owned the world.

One night when we were sneaking in, a big guy grabbed Kenny. We started to run, but we could not leave Kenny. The guy said, "I am the new guard and I will call the police." We begged him, "Please don't call the police, we are only poor kids from the neighborhood. We don't have money for movie tickets and we don't have a car."

He looked at us and said, "No, I guess eleven-year-old kids don't have a car. So I will tell you something. From now on I will let you into the movie free, but you have to come around to the front and leave your bikes at the ticket booth. Tell the lady selling tickets that you are my guests. My name is Bill."

From then on, we entered through the entrance as friends of Bill. We felt very proud. Now we really did own the world.

MONEYMAKING SCHEMES

Poor kids do not get weekly allowances. It is not due to lack of love, but lack of money.

This did not bother Kenny and me. This was simply a small hurdle to overcome.

We devised ways to make money. We watched what others did, and learned a lot from them. Often, we thought that evangelists had some of the best schemes.

We never lacked for sodas, candy, or new ornaments for our bicycles. We were young entrepreneurs.

How to Make Money

Kenny and I knew how to make money. We rode our bikes along the road and watched for cold drink bottles that people had thrown from their cars. It amazed us that people threw away their money. We took along an old bag that oranges came in to hold the bottles. In order to buy a candy bar and a cold drink, we each needed to pick up five bottles. Each bottle was worth two cents at Mr. Lacky's store. He was also our school bus driver.

Candy bars were a nickel. Cold drinks were a nickel, too. We always bought the biggest soda we could get for a nickel. Pepsi Cola was twice as big as Coca Cola, which had only six ounces. So did Dr. Pepper. My Aunt Ola said that Dr. Pepper was much better for us because a doctor invented it. She also said you should drink it three times a day, at 10 o'clock and 2 o'clock and 4 o'clock just like it said on the bottle.

We didn't care if Dr. Pepper was better for us. Pepsi Cola had twelve ounces. Sometimes we bought a little bag of peanuts instead of candy. We would drink a little of our Pepsi, then pour the bag of peanuts into our cold drink. It was great. I wondered if other kids knew about pouring peanuts into their cold drinks. We had to drink our Pepsi outside Mr. Lacky's store and leave the bottle with him before we left because that bottle would cost us two cents if we took it with us.

Popular Mechanics magazine always had a lot of really neat classified ads. We found one that said, "Make Money Selling Flower and Vegetable Seeds." Kenny and I thought about it. It was early spring and if we ordered soon, we would have the seeds in time to sell to our neighbors. Over the next week, we rode our bikes along the highways and collected three dollars worth of bottles. We sent away for the seeds. We watched each day for the rural mailman's car to come over the hill.

The seeds finally arrived on Monday. We were very excited. By Friday we would be rich, or at least not have to pick up cold drink bottles to sell for candy.

We opened the box and we had seeds, seeds, and more seeds. The packages were beautiful. There were pictures of all kinds of flowers and vegetables too.

We took our new supply of seeds to Granny Paulson's house. I told Kenny that I knew she would want to buy some. She was the one who always let us climb her apple tree for green apples.

Granny said she did not need any seeds right now. We learned that "right now" probably really meant never.

So we went from one poor neighbor's house to the next and found that no one needed seeds.

We asked Momma if she wanted to buy some seeds. She did not have the money either, so we gave her the seeds.

Later we had really pretty flowers in our yard. Momma was happy.

We went back to picking up cold drink bottles.

Prayer Changes Things

Most of our neighbors were religious people, born again, conservative fundamentalists and God-fearing. They had a simple faith, and believed in prayer and Mr. Roosevelt.

After Kenny and I failed at selling seeds, I thought of a new idea that I was sure would work. Granny Paulson had a beautiful blue card hanging on her wall that, in silver glitter sparkling letters said, *Prayer Changes Things*. I asked her where she got it. She told me that she saw it advertised in a magazine and sent for it. The card cost fifty cents. She was quite proud of it.

We looked in Popular Mechanics magazine. They had hundreds of little ads. We found one that said, *Make Money, Sell Beautiful Christian Heartfelt Wall Messages that are Suitable for Framing. Makes any home glow with Christian warmth.*

It said that we could buy twenty cards for twenty-five cents each and sell them to our neighbors and loved ones for fifty cents each. We would make five dollars profit by selling only twenty cards.

We went through the list of sayings from the company and picked out ones that we thought would tug at the heartstrings: *Prayer Changes Things, We Love Jesus, Jesus is in this House, Home Sweet Home* and *The Old Rugged Cross*. Kenny felt the *Old Rugged Cross* would be a winner for sure.

We spent the next two weeks picking up cold drink bottles along the road. We took them to Mr. Lacky's store to collect the five dollars we needed for the lovely heartfelt wall decorations. Mr. Lacky asked,

"What are you going to do with all that money?" We told him we were going to use it to go into a business of our own.

We put five one-dollar bills in an envelope and addressed it and waited for the mailman to drive up to our mailbox. We were excited. Kenny said, "We should have a little prayer before we sent all that money in the mail." He prayed, "Jesus, please protect our money so we can be rich."

In about a week, the mailman drove up in his ugly Nash car, smiled and handed us a cardboard box. We ran to the house and opened it. It had twenty beautiful blue 8 x 10-inch cards with silver glitter letters. They would be lovely in any Christian home that loved Jesus.

We walked to our neighbors with our box full of cards that would make even a sinner's home seem religious.

The neighbors loved them. Even the ones who did not buy our seeds loved them. Some bought two cards, one for the living room and one to hang over their bed. It did not take much imagination for us to realize that these beautiful sayings hanging on the walls would beautify any living room.

We sold out in two days.

We learned that Prayer Did Change Things. It made us rich.

Selling Watermelons

A friend, who lived in town, asked if I missed not getting an allowance each week. I told him you don't miss something you have never had.

I knew it was good to have a little money to spend. That was why Kenny and I worked out a number of ways to make money.

We were always watching for new ways to make some change.

Mr. Winger had a large watermelon field that bordered our land. He was very protective of his melons. On several occasions we heard gunfire at night when he caught kids trying to steal his watermelons.

He would fire over their heads to scare them. After he shot, we would hear kids trying to run away and hear them scream as they got tangled in the barbed wire fence that he had around three sides of the patch.

He gave Kenny and me permission to go into his field during the day to eat as many watermelons as we wanted. He liked us.

One day he said, "If you boys want to make a few dollars, you should set up a watermelon stand on Congo Road." We said, "Good idea–How much do we have to pay you for the watermelons?" He surprised us. He said, "You boys can take five melons from my patch and when you sell them, come back for five more, and so on." He said he liked to see people try to make money. He did not like kids stealing from him. He said, "I am not going to charge you anything as long as you don't give any away."

We found some boards and nails. We got an old piece of tarpaulin for our roof. We built a pretty nice stand right up by the curve on Congo Road. We put up a sign that said:

WATERMELONS for a QUARTER, ANY SIZE!

We went to the field with my little red wagon. The watermelon field was close to the curve where we set up our stand. We picked five melons of various sizes and put them in the wagon. We went back to the stand and set them on the shelf.

It went very slow at first. Not many cars went by. Then people started to pass by on their way home from work. The first car to stop was a red convertible. The man looked over our melons. He wanted to buy two, one large and one smaller one. He handed us a dollar bill. Kenny looked at me and I looked at him. We did not have any change. We had not even thought of needing change.

The man said, "I can see I am your first customer today. Don't worry. I will stop by tomorrow and you can give me my change then." He trusted us. That was nice. We assured him that tomorrow we would have his change ready.

The next person bought two. We had only one more melon to sell. I sent Kenny to the field to get more melons. Kenny was so excited that he almost forgot to take the wagon. I told him to hurry, but to be sure to select good melons and not turn the wagon over on his way back.

We sold three more that first day. We had to take the other three melons back to our house for the night. We did not want other kids stealing our three watermelons.

When we got back to the house we were excited to tell Momma and Daddy that we had sold seven watermelons on our first day of sales. Daddy said, "That is great. Now you should go right over to Mr. Winger and give him your report on sales and thank him."

We did and Mr. Winger seemed impressed. He said, "You can do the same again tomorrow. Save your money and someday you might own your own watermelon patch." We said, "Thank you, sir–It is very thoughtful of you." (I had heard my Daddy say that to someone once and I thought it sounded grown-up.)

I did not see myself owning a watermelon patch in my future, but I did see a brand-new bicycle with a horn, lights and mud flaps as a possibility. Kenny did, too.

The next day the red convertible pulled up to our stand. The man got out and came over. We had two quarters waiting for him. I held them out to him. He said, "No, I do not want the money. I want two more watermelons."

We were thrilled. We already had a return customer.

Playing Records Without a Record Player

Momma and Daddy had an old Victrola record player. It had a handle on the side, which you had to wind to make it play.

We had always been told not to wind it too tight or we might break the spring. We did. It broke. Daddy was not happy with Kenny and me for breaking the Victrola. He said, "I hope you two have learned your lesson! Now you will not be able to listen to Jimmy Durante or any of the other music people."

We were upset that we could no longer hear the music. We thought about it for a while. We knew that the needle sat in the groove of the record and when the record went around, somehow music went through the needle and into the horn-style speaker.

I went to the kitchen, got the broom and took a straw from it. I told Kenny to turn the record by hand as fast as he could. I held the broom straw between my fingers and placed the straw gently down in the groove. Kenny turned. We heard nothing.

Then I thought, "What if I hold the straw not between my fingers, but between my front teeth, then put the straw down in the groove while Kenny turns the record." Suddenly, I could hear a little music. I grinned at Kenny. He wanted a turn. I said, "Wait, lets put our fingers in our ears and see if we can hear better." We could! It worked great! Then, I turned the record and Kenny listened.

Kenny said, "This has great moneymaking possibilities! We can make money from our friends by letting them listen for a nickel." "Good idea," I said, "but let's make them each turn the record before they get to hear the music."

Before long, word got out along Congo Road that Clyde and Kenny had made a new discovery. Kids brought their nickels. Then we discovered that they would pay a penny just to get to turn the records. Man we were hauling in the money at six cents per play!

As Daddy said, we learned our lesson.

Drowning Flies

I can't remember how we knew that you could drown a housefly and bring it back to life, but we did. We would carefully catch a fly with our hands, then hold it under water and drown it. Then we would cover the fly with salt, wait a few minutes, and soon you would see one wing flutter a little, then the other wing would flutter. In a few minutes the fly would shake itself and fly away.

I told Kenny that I thought it should be worth a nickel for a kid to see a miracle performed. He grinned. So, we had kids pay a nickel to watch. We drowned a fly, and then brought it back to life. A miracle performed right before their eyes. They were so impressed, and we made fifty-five cents.

The next week the Bible teacher in church told about Jesus bringing Lazarus back to life. We told the teacher that we could bring things back to life, too.

She thought we were sacrilegious. She jumped down our throats and told us we should be ashamed for saying such things. We kept our mouths shut after that. We never did show the teacher that we could perform miracles, too. She would just have to go through life without seeing a miracle performed. She had her chance.

Selling Christmas Trees and Roman Candles

My older married brother, Willy, asked Kenny and me if we would like to help him sell Christmas trees. We said, "Sure we would love to help."

In the past, we had helped Willy dig worms from under soaked leaves along the river bottom. When you pulled the leaves back, there would be hundreds of them. We would sometimes uncover snakes, and that was scary. Willy would sell the worms, which we called night crawlers, to a local bait shop for a penny each. We would dig five hundred worms and get five dollars. That was a lot of work for only five dollars. Willy did this work to help supplement his small income that he made at The Jones Furniture Manufacturing Company in town.

Selling Christmas trees sounded a lot better to us than digging worms.

Willy had gone into the woods and cut a number of cedar trees. We were going to sell them out of the back of his old Plymouth station wagon and an old trailer. The NAPA auto store had given him permission to use their parking lot after closing each day, as well as on Sundays.

Willy thought we also should try selling some fireworks. A lot of people in Arkansas shot fireworks at Christmas, New Year's Eve, and the Fourth of July. Willy said his brother-in-law was a firework wholesaler, so we could buy them from him.

About ten days before Christmas we set up our display and started to sell Christmas trees. We priced the trees two dollars and fifty cents each. We also had several different types of fireworks to sell.

I said to Willy, "Why don't we include a Roman candle with each tree for free?"

Willy looked at me and said, "Then we are only getting two dollars for each tree if we give away a Roman candle that sells for fifty cents. That is not a good deal for us."

I said, "No, we can charge three dollars for our trees and that includes a free Roman candle. They will go for it, I am sure. Everyone likes a *free* deal."

Willy said, "But our competitor down the street is selling his trees for two fifty, which is fifty cents less. The customers will go there for their trees."

I said, "People like to get something free. I learned this from the tent evangelist who offered folks a free Bible if they attended his tent meetings for four out of five nights. It worked for him and I am sure it will work for us."

So Willy gave in and said he was willing to let us try it for a while. We tied a Roman candle to the top of each tree. We pointed out to our customers that they were getting a Roman candle with their tree purchase.

A couple of days later, a big heavy man in a suit and tie stopped by to look at our trees. He said that he was a preacher at one of the Baptist Churches in town. He had seen our sign that said *"Christmas Trees with a free Roman Candle - Celebrate Christmas."*

He told us that we were not being very Christian, offering our trees, to celebrate the birth of Jesus, with a Roman candle as a come-on for a sale.

This took us by surprise. Willy looked at me. Kenny looked at me. I looked at the preacher. The "free Roman candle" was my idea, so I was supposed to come up with an answer.

I said, "Well, sir, the Bible says that as Jesus lay in the manger, a bright star shined down on his birthplace. It brought the wise men to worship him." "Yes, that is correct," the preacher said. I said, "Well, sir, we do not have a shining star to celebrate the birth of Jesus, but we do have Roman candles. If you buy a tree, you get a free candle."

Then I said, "You can go outside on Christmas Eve, fire off your Roman candle and let your neighbors know that you and your family are celebrating Jesus' birth."

He looked at me, then Willy, then Kenny, then back to me. He said, "Son, I like that. I really like that. In fact, I would like to use it in my sermon this coming Sunday. Do you mind if I do?"

I said, "No, sir, we are happy to help you spread the good word to all your neighbors."

When he left, Willy said, "How did you ever come up with all that?"

I just grinned. I had learned some things from the tent evangelist.

I said, "We had better have a few extra trees and Roman Candles on hand next Sunday afternoon in case he uses my story in his sermon."

On Sunday, after church, cars started pulling into our parking lot. People were telling us the wonderful story Pastor Smith had told them. They too, wanted to share their faith. Some already had a tree at home, but they wanted to have one of those special Roman candles that Pastor Smith had held up in church for all to see.

Kenny started to say, "They are not special, they are just Roman candles." I stopped Kenny and said, "Yes, Kenny, they are special when people want them to be special. They want them for a special purpose."

We sold everything we had in about thirty minutes. We said we would be back, again tomorrow evening, with more trees and Roman candles. "Be sure and tell your neighbors," we said.

That Christmas the sale of Christmas trees went very well. We made a lot of people feel very special, and we made a lot of money helping them feel that way.

My Artistic Beginnings

My interest in art goes back as far as I can remember. My mother bought crayons and gave me scrap paper to work on. I remember lying on a quilt blanket pallet (as we called it) on the floor and coloring and drawing in the light of oil lamps before we got electricity in our house.

One day I was visiting my Aunt Ola and she allowed me to go up into her attic. There I discovered beautiful oil paintings that had been painted by someone in her family. Right in that attic, when I was seven years old, I knew what I wanted to be in life.

I also had a teacher in church school to whom I am indebted–Miss Winter, a very strange, but friendly woman. She introduced me to pastels, and gave me a box of them.

Several years later, when I was eleven years old, my Aunt Ola's son, Aubry Coleman, a well-known landscape painter in Arkansas, taught me to paint.

I was determined not to work in the Bauxite Mines, as did a lot of others I grew up with. I was going to be an artist!

An Important Discovery in Aunt Ola's Attic

I loved to visit my Aunt Ola. She is my Momma's half sister. She lived up Congo Road about three miles from our house. Her husband, Uncle Judd, had money. He owned a sawmill and made all kinds of handles for tools on his big wood lathes.

They had an indoor bathroom with a large bathtub. I liked to use their toilet but she never asked me if I wanted to take a bath in her tub. It was just for the two of them, I thought.

Aunt Ola also had an attic with a staircase. When I visited her, she always gave me Graham Crackers and a Dr. Pepper cold drink. She said they were both healthy. Then I would head to the attic. The things that fascinated me most were some very old oil paintings. One was a *Snow scene with a wolf howling at the moon*. Another favorite was a *River with a Cabin* beside it.

Those two paintings made me want to be an artist. Aunt Ola said, "Art talent runs in the family." Her son, Aubry, was a wonderful landscape painter. I hoped the talent would "run" in me, too.

When I got back home I told my Momma that I had seen those beautiful paintings. I said, "I want to learn how to paint and be an artist." She said, "Oil paints are pretty expensive, but I will see what I can do."

She wrote a letter to my sister, Sue, who was recently married. Sue now lived in San Antonio, Texas with her husband, Marvin who was in the Army. He did not have to go to the battlefield because he had a much more important job to do for the army. He painted glass eyes for the soldiers who had an eye shot out. And, they used tubes of oil paint to paint the glass eyes.

He said, "I think I can 'borrow' a few old tubes from the army." He sent me quite a selection of partially used tubes of oil paint. I could not believe it.

Momma took me to Little Rock to look for an easel. We found a wooden one for five dollars. I asked Momma, "Can we afford an expensive easel like this?" She said, "I have saved some money for it." We brought it home.

Now all I needed was canvas. Daddy said he had some old green cloth canvas roll-up window shades in the attic. We climbed the ladder to our little attic and got the shades. Daddy and I made a stretcher out of wood and I tacked the window shade canvas to the stretcher, just like the old masters did. I think they had better canvas though.

I started to paint what I thought were beautiful paintings. Momma, Daddy and Kenny said they were great! What more could a young artist ask. It "runs in the family," you know.

My New Crayolas

One day my Momma surprised me with a new box of Crayolas. It was a big box with 48 different colors in it. There were variations of blues and greens and even purples. One color that I found interesting was named Flesh.

In church we had learned a little song that said, "*Jesus loves the little children, all the children of the world. Red and yellow, black and white, all are precious in his sight.*" Now this made me wonder: Does the Crayola Company make different *flesh colors* for all these different children that Jesus loves? And how do kids know which box to choose from the store shelf? Crayola should have printed on the outside of the box: *Contains Yellow Flesh color or Colored Flesh color or Red Flesh color or White Flesh color.*

Maybe Crayola does sell different flesh colors in the big cities. I thought they should.

The Box of Pastels

My love for art was growing. I drew a lot and painted every chance I had. I loved Prang watercolors in the long black tin box. They were the best, and had the brightest colors.

Miss Winter, my fifth grade teacher, who looked like winter with her white skin and white hair, encouraged me to do art. She told me that she had some pastel colored chalk. She wanted to know if I would like for her to teach me the technique.

She opened her box of pastels. They were beautiful. She also had some special paper for the pastel drawings. It was large, about 11" by 14". She had some pretty pictures that she saved from greeting cards. I chose one to copy.

She allowed me to continue doing pastel drawings during two class periods. I loved it. I did not miss not having science and math class that day.

After about two hours I had completed a beautiful pastel of flowers. Miss Winter was so pleased. She had some old frames. She said we could put the art into one of them. I took it home for Momma.

Momma could not believe that I had done it all by myself. She immediately took down the Ashby Funeral Home calendar and hung my picture in its place in the living room. It looked great with her new linoleum that she was so proud of. She said, "We will save and buy you a box of pastels when we go back to Little Rock."

I had tried my hand at watercolor, oil paint and now pastels. I liked all of them. I was on the way to becoming an artist. I was not going to farm or work in the Bauxite mines as a lot of the kids do after high school.

I started to think more about what Aunt Ola told me about art talent "running in our family." I was going to be an artist.

Art Lessons

Aubry Coleman was my Aunt Ola's son. He was also my cousin, but he did not seem like one to me. He was about thirty years old and I was eleven. He heard about my interest in art from Aunt Ola. She had bragged about me a little, I was sure.

Aubry was a very well-known landscape painter in Arkansas. He sold his paintings for a lot of money. He also had classes for kids in his neighborhood. He taught art lessons in his home in Benton.

He asked me if I would like to take his art classes. I said, "Yes, I would love that."

He knew about "our being a little short of money," as Daddy says. He said, "You are my cousin, so I want to offer the classes free to you."

I thanked him for his kindness. I realized the meaning of the "cousin and free" thing, but I did not let on. I appreciated the way he made his offer.

I did not have a way to get into town on Tuesday evenings for the lessons. If the classes were in the daytime, I could have ridden my bike. Uncle Judd offered to pick me up and carry me to Aubry's each week. He said we could get a Dairy Queen on the way home. That sounded great.

There were six boys in the class. I did not know the others. I liked them. Aubry gave each student three pencils and a pad of drawing paper. My favorite pencil was an Ebony Pencil. It had soft lead.

He taught us how to do shading of tree leaves, which made them look real. He taught us perspective. It was wonderful to learn how to make things look smaller as they went into the background of your drawing.

We met for several weeks. We were all getting better at drawing. Then he started to teach us to paint with oils. He showed us some of his work. They were beautiful. I could see how people would pay a lot of money to own one of his paintings. I wished I could buy one.

He said that before we started to paint, he thought we should visit a real art museum and look at a lot of paintings by various painters. He said, "We will go to Little Rock next Sunday afternoon." He had a station wagon and we all piled in. I was thrilled. I had never been to a museum before. Some of the other boys had.

As we arrived at the museum grounds, I saw large statues of men on horses. They all looked like someone had poured a greenish paint on them. I was very upset seeing this. I said, "Look, someone poured paint on the statues!" Some of the boys, who had been there before, started to laugh at me. They said, "Clyde, that is not paint. That is patina. That naturally happens due to weather." I did not know anything about patina. Aubry, realized my situation, said, "I think that is very good that Clyde is concerned about the art work." That seemed to hush the other boys.

As we walked into the large building, I was shocked. Up on the wall, right in front of us was a painting, about eight feet long. It was of a beautiful naked woman, lying down. I was flabbergasted. I had never seen a full-grown naked woman before. I loved it, but was afraid to know why. Was it the beautiful paint, or the pose or just that she was so naked? Whatever it was, I knew I wanted to be an artist, right then and there, for sure. Some of the other boys snickered. I did not.

We spent about two hours in the museum. We saw many wonderful paintings. When we got into Aubry's car to return home, he asked us what we liked the best. I said, "I liked the naked woman the best of all." He smiled and said, "Yes, she was naked, but in art, we call that Nude."

Not only had I learned about painting that day, but I had learned a new word that I can use forever–a good one, too.

I came back inspired. When I got home, Momma asked me to tell her about everything that we saw at the museum. She had never been to a museum either.

I told her about the beautiful landscapes, the lovely still lifes, and the portraits, but I did not mention the wonderful nude woman. Momma was pretty rigid about such things. It was best for her if I just kept this to myself. Someday I might tell her, but not now. I wanted to keep taking art lessons.

THE COLORED SITUATION

As a child, it was interesting growing up in the South. One learns a lot, develops a lot of questions and seeks answers.

My Father and Mother were born in the South, learned Southern traditions and did not question them. Neither of my parents had gone beyond the eighth grade in school, which was the case with a lot of poor people in those days.

My Father would use the word "nigger" without a thought as to what he was saying. My mother had more respect, I think due to her church influence, so she used the word "nigra," thinking that was more respectful.

As a kid, I thought that we should use the word colored. I reasoned that they were colored and we were white. It was very simple to my way of thinking. People are taught that traditions are sacred, without thought to where those originated. This was the way it was in the South in the 1940s and early 1950s. But times were starting to change, and quickly.

The Truckload of Mexicans

Kenny and I were at Mr. Lacky's store buying cold drinks when a large truck pulled into the drive. It had a canvas tent-like covering over the back. The driver came into the store and told Mr. Lacky that he needed gas and wanted to use the restroom.

Mr. Lacky said, "What do you have in the truck?" The man answered in broken English that he had a truckload of Mexicanos. He said he was taking them up to Michigan to pick fruit. Mr. Lacky said, "You can buy gas and you can buy them all a cold drink, but they cannot use my restroom. They can use the woods out back, but the restrooms are for white customers only."

The Mexican man said, "Yes, I have been told this along the road, all the way through Texas and now in Arkansas. I don't think you people like Mexicanos." Mr. Lacky said, "No, it is not that we don't like Mexicans, it's just that you are not white and we have to preserve our beliefs." The Mexican looked at him and said, "OK."

The man went to the back of the truck and unhooked the tarp so the Mexicans could get out of the truck. There must have been about 25 of them–women, men and some children. Kenny and I had never been close to a Mexican before and we were very curious. There was a boy and a girl about our age. They seemed very shy. Kenny and I were not shy. We went over and said, "Hi, what are your names?" They both just looked at us and seemed a bit scared. The boy said something to the girl, but we could not understand. We realized that they could not speak English and we could not speak Mexican.

All the Mexicans started for the woods, and some seemed to be in a hurry. We did not follow them, but we were curious how that was going to work, with men and women all back there together.

When they came back from the woods, they all went into the store. The driver, who seemed to be the boss man, bought each one of them a cold drink. Kenny and I had some penny candy and we gave some to the boy and girl. They smiled and said something like "grasseus." We smiled back. We smiled at the rest of them–some smiled and some did not.

They all climbed back into the truck. The driver began to close the tarp. We waved goodbye to them and they all waved back. The truck pulled away.

We went back inside and told Mr. Lacky that we thought they seemed nice–even if they were not white, they were not colored. He said, "They are always very nice when they stop by, but I cannot have my neighbors see me letting them use my restrooms. I have to protect my business, and they would use a lot of my toilet paper, too."

We rode home on our bikes. Kenny said he could not understand everything that had just happened. I said we would ask Daddy about it when we get home. We told him what we had just seen at Mr. Lacky's. We asked him to explain why it is that only whites have the right to use restrooms and drinking fountains.

Daddy said, "Well, there are a lot of examples of whites in the Bible. It says we are made in God's image and he is white." He then said "Adam and Eve were white as well as Noah and King David and Solomon and John the Baptist and Jesus, too. They say Jesus was a Jew, but we live with that. None of them in the Bible were colored or wetbacks or Japs." We asked him what wetbacks were. He said, "That is what you saw at Mr. Lacky's, they are Mexicans and are called that because many of them swim the Rio Grand River to get into the United States illegally."

We asked Daddy where all the other non-white people come from. He said, "I don't know, but I know there is nothing said about them in the Bible. Even Santa Claus is white, whether you kids believe in him anymore or not."

Daddy said that people in the south have always been taught that white people are superior to all the other races, and that Southerners are just trying to stick to the traditions that they have been taught from birth.

Kenny and I had learned a lot that day, including the fact that we were very lucky to have been born white, like God, even if we don't have a lot of money and "worldly goods" as the preacher says.

We could drink from any drinking fountain that we wished to.

Daddy, and The Colored

One day when Daddy and I were in town, we saw a colored man that Daddy liked. He worked at the Ford garage. He did the sweeping and made things look nice.

Daddy called him "Hot." In fact everyone called him "Hot." No one seemed to know why. They just did. Hot called my Daddy, "Mista Mac." They talked for a while, then Daddy and I went to pay the electric bill.

As we walked, I asked Daddy why he did not like colored people, but he did like Hot. He thought about it for a while. He said, "Well, when I was young I was taught not to like niggers and I guess it has stayed with me. I was taught, however, that you could like some of them, even as friends."

I told him that I heard at school that we should not call them niggers. We should show respect and call them nigras. I also heard that they should be called negroes. I didn't think either of those words sounded very respectful. I thought the word "colored" sounded the most respectful. I said, "They are colored and we are white. Maybe we should call them brown. Us white and them brown. Doesn't that make sense?"

He did not say much. In a few minutes he said, "I would be happy to have Hot and his wife over for supper sometime. I also like Tom, the colored man who works at the Alcoa plant. He has always been nice to me."

After that, I never talked to Daddy about the colored situation in the South. He seemed uneasy about the subject. Things were starting to change and I think a lot of southern white people were starting to get concerned. There was some unrest in the colored community and Daddy told me never to go across the railroad tracks to where they lived. He said it could be dangerous for a white boy.

I listened. I did not go across the tracks.

Visit to Aunt Madeline's in Memphis

The last time Aunt Madeline and Uncle Marvin visited us, she pulled me up close and told me, "I think that since you are now eight years old, you should come to Memphis to visit us." She thought that a week in July, when school is out for the summer, would be good for my cousin Barry and me. Barry and his folks lived with Aunt Madeline and Uncle Marvin. I had never been to Memphis before and had never met Barry.

This was exciting to me, but scary as well. I had never been away from home. My Momma said it would be all right if we had the money for a bus ticket. Memphis is a big city and it is about three hours away. Aunt Madeline said, "I will be happy to pay for the bus tickets both ways." We all agreed that the middle of July would be a good time for the trip.

Aunt Madeline told Momma, "Be sure he has clean underwear and socks, and be sure not to send any Arkansas ticks along in his clothes." Aunt Madeline seemed very worried about germs.

The only time I had been on a big Greyhound bus was five years ago when Momma and I went to Hot Springs when Kenny was born. I was starting to get pretty nervous about the idea of traveling alone. How would I know if the bus was headed in the right direction? How would I know when the bus got to Memphis and what if I got off at the wrong town? What if someone wanted to kidnap a skinny kid like me?

Momma assured me that she would talk to the bus driver and have him look out for me. She said, "Aunt Madeline will be at the Memphis bus station waiting for you." I knew if she was there that I would be able to spot her, short, round and with big bosoms, not to mention the black hair sticking out of the mole on her pointed chin.

Finally the big day arrived. I had my little suitcase packed with my clean pair of socks and underwear. I said goodbye to Kenny. He was not old enough to go. I hugged Momma and Daddy and suddenly was not so sure I wanted to see the big city. How would my folks get along without me?

The bus door opened and a nice smiling man with a little hat with a bill on it said, "Going to Memphis?" My Momma went in ahead of me and told him about my situation. He promised her that he would be the driver all the way to Memphis, and there would be only one stop that we would make, at a bus station that had a restaurant in it. He would be sure that I got back on the right bus. He said that he would not leave me until Aunt Madeline was there to pick me up. He also said I could sit on the very first seat close to him on the bus. That made me feel a lot better.

Momma gave me a couple of dollars to buy a sandwich and a Pepsi when we came to the bus station with the restaurant. I hugged Momma a really long time.

Soon the bus started to fill with other riders. I kept my little suitcase on the seat beside me so no one would sit with me.

Several white passengers boarded the bus. Most of them gave me a big smile. None of them looked like kidnappers.

Then the colored riders started to board the bus. They also gave me big smiles. I had never been close to a smiling colored person before. They all seemed to have big white teeth. I noticed that the white passenger's teeth were not as white, but more yellow. I wondered how colored people could have such white teeth and white people have such yellow teeth. It did not make sense to me.

The colored people all went to the back of the bus. There were empty rows of seats closer to the front, but they did not stop at them. There was a small colored boy, a bit younger than me, with his Momma. I motioned for him to come and sit with me. He looked at his Momma and she said no. He had to sit in the back with her. She smiled at me though. She had bright white teeth, too.

The bus driver was very nice to me and asked me a million questions. He kept my mind from thinking about how I was sure my parents were going to have a hard time with me being gone.

After about an hour and a half we arrived at the bus station with the restaurant, which was about half way to Memphis. The bus driver told me to wait until he got the other passengers off the bus, then he would take me inside. Soon everyone was off the bus and the driver and I went inside.

I needed a drink of water. There were two drinking fountains standing side by side, about two feet apart. Over one fountain the sign said, "Colored." Over the other fountain the sign said, "Whites Only." I had never seen anything like this in our small hometown. I obeyed the signs.

Then the bus driver guided me to the eating area with the stools at the counter. Over the counter was another sign that said "Whites Only." There were stoves for cooking the food. On the other side of the stoves was a smaller counter with stools that said, "Colored."

The driver and I sat at the large counter. The cooks were colored but they served both the colored and the white customers. This was all so new to me. You very seldom saw colored people in my little town, so I guessed the signs were not necessary there.

We finished, and everyone climbed back on the bus smelling like southern fried chicken.

We drove across the Arkansas Delta. I saw field after field of people picking cotton. All the cotton pickers were colored, both men and women and kids pulling long white sacks behind them. They kept pushing the handpicked cotton down into the large white bags. There was a white man standing by the wagon where the sacks were dumped. I thought he was the boss man.

Along all of the fields were little rows of small wooden houses. You could see through the cracks in the walls. Very old looking colored people sat around on the porch fanning themselves with their straw hats and little paper fans. Smaller colored kids were playing in the dirt around and under the little houses. Sometimes there would be a poor looking cow tied to the corner of the house with a bucket of water sitting nearby.

Then we came to the swampy area where the Cyprus trees grew. There were lots of wild poisonous snakes out there, I knew. I hoped the bus did not get a flat tire in that scary swamp.

A few more miles and the driver said to me, "Be watching for the huge bridge ahead. It goes over the great Mississippi River which separates Arkansas from Tennessee." I could see it above the treetops and soon we were flying over the river below. I could hardly catch my breath.

A little later we pulled into the huge bus station. There were buses everywhere. People everywhere. Loudspeakers blaring out *St. Louis, Chicago, Nashville, Chattanooga* and a thousand more places. The place was too big. Aunt Madeline would never find me in this mob. I knew I might have to live in this bus station the rest of my life if she could not find me.

The bus stopped and the door opened. I grabbed my suitcase and asked the driver, "What do I do now?" He said, "Let me get all the people off the bus and then we will look for Aunt Madeline." He started helping everyone off the bus and I spied my Aunt Madeline waving to our bus. She was there for me. She came over and grabbed me and pulled me into her big bosoms. I simply held my breath and closed my eyes. For some reason she did not smell so funny this time.

She already had a doctor's appointment set for me for the next morning. She said that since I had been living and playing with Kenny that she wanted me to be tested. She wanted to be sure I did not have the TB germ. Kenny, his Momma and Daddy had all had TB two years before. Kenny and his Momma were cured, but his Daddy had died.

Fortunately I passed the TB test and could now play with my cousin Barry. Barry was a bit sickly and a bit of a sissy. He knew how to hold his fork just right when eating, and to keep his feet on the floor. Boy, I did not know any of the strange rules of Aunt Madeline's. This fussy stuff was not what I was used to. I was not sure if she was going to be able to put up with me for a whole week. I missed my Momma and Daddy. Aunt Madeline's rules made sense to her, but not to me. They were sure weird.

Barry asked me if I liked to watch the Howdy Doody Show on the television set. I had no idea about what he meant about Howdy Doody or television. He said, "You don't have television in Arkansas?" I said, "No, I guess not, since I don't know what it is."

He took me into the living room and turned a knob on a thing larger than a radio but with a glass front. Pretty soon the glass lit up and a black and white picture came on like small pictures at the movies.

It was time for a guy named Buffalo Bob and a dumb wooden puppet named Howdy. Buffalo Bob wore a western type of shirt with buckskin fringe hanging down from his sleeves. He talked to Howdy, the puppet.

When the Howdy Doody Show was over, Aunt Madeline came in and turned off the television and said "That is all the TV you can watch today."

I went to sleep that night wondering if we would ever get television in Arkansas. That made me think about my Momma and Daddy and how sad they were that I was not there with them.

But I was willing to stay another day, because before we went to bed, Aunt Madeline told us, "Tomorrow the ice cream man will come down the street and you can each buy an ice cream bar."

Yes, I could stay at least another day in Memphis. I loved ice cream.

Becoming a Junior Deputy Sheriff

A new man was running for sheriff for our county. His name was Jim Johnson. He was a Democrat, so Daddy thought he was all right.

Daddy and I went to one of his campaign speeches on the courthouse steps.

He was a tall man, with a white cowboy hat and a big smile. I thought he would make a fine sheriff. When he started speaking, he said something that really got my attention. He said, "We have a lot of good kids in our county. I am going to make each young man in Saline County a Junior Deputy Sheriff during my first year in Office. Once I am elected, I will open my office the first Saturday and have every white boy between ten and sixteen years of age who wants to be a Junior Deputy Sheriff come by, sign up and receive a real metal Junior Deputy Sheriff's badge."

He got a big round of applause. I clapped the loudest. I told my Daddy, "You have to vote for Jim Johnson, you have to help him get elected. By electing him, you will be electing me, too, as a Junior Deputy Sheriff. We have never had a sheriff in the family."

Daddy promised me that he was going to vote for him. Daddy said, "He is up against the current sheriff and he is a Republican." I said, "We Democrats can whip him. I know we can." Then I said, "Daddy, I think he could get a lot of the colored people to vote for him if they could. If the colored didn't have to pay the two-dollar poll tax, they could vote too." Daddy did not say anything.

After Jim Johnson was through speaking, I went up to him and said, "How can I help with your election, Mr. Johnson?" He looked at me and said, "What is your name, boy, and how old are you?" I told him my name and that I was eleven years old. He asked if I could help put flyers on the doors of houses in Benton the night before the election. He said there would be some of his people that would take kids to different parts of town to distribute the flyers. I told him I would be happy to help him get elected.

The night before election, about twenty of us kids arrived to distribute flyers to help elect Jim Johnson as Sheriff of Saline County.

The next day was Election Day. When the polls closed, Jim Johnson was elected the new Sheriff of Saline County. I was very proud to help get him elected. Now I was going to get to be a Junior Deputy Sheriff. I could not wait for the first Saturday of his term in office.

My Momma said, "I hope the swearing-in is not on Saturday morning during church service." I thought, "Oh, no. This could be a problem." Kenny was concerned for me, and my problem. He was eight years old, not old enough to be a Junior Deputy. He said, "I think it will work out for you. The Lord needs a good boy like you to wear the badge."

A few weeks later, the newspaper said that on Thursday the new Sheriff was to be sworn into office. This was exciting since Saturday he would be swearing in all of us Junior Deputies. The paper said the swearing in for the Junior Deputy Sheriffs was to be at 2:00 pm, Saturday, at the Sheriff's Office.

Daddy showed Kenny and me the newspaper. I was delighted. Kenny said, "I knew it would work out for you." He was right again.

There were about a hundred of us white boys between ten and sixteen years old at the swearing-in ceremonies. Most were nearer my age. Sheriff Johnson stood in front of us and gave us a big smile. I think he knew this Junior Deputy idea had helped him get elected.

He told us that we had to uphold the law, report any crimes we saw committed and be nice to the citizens of our county. He said for us to line up. He was going to personally pin the new badges on each one of us.

He started down the line. I was about fifth in line. When he came to me, he said, "Well, Clyde, your hard work distributing those flyers got me elected. Thank you for helping and thank you for volunteering to be one of my Deputies." You could have knocked me over with a broom straw. He remembered my name! I could not believe it.

Momma and Daddy were watching from the back of the room. They each had a big grin on their face. Kenny was there too, proudly waving at me–his uncle, Clyde McCulley, Junior Deputy Sheriff of Saline County, Arkansas.

I told Momma, Daddy and Kenny, "Now that I am a genuine Junior Deputy Sheriff, hopefully I can help get that poll tax changed. Then the poor whites and the poor colored can vote, too. I wonder why he did not want any colored boys to be his Deputy Sheriffs."

Daddy just gave a half smile, but said nothing.

Early Morning Radio

My Daddy always listened to early morning radio from a radio station somewhere in Texas. First came the weather report, then some country music including some from a new country star named Hank Williams. I liked him a lot. I had first heard him sing on the jukebox at the Triangle Cafe a few weeks ago.

After the country music program there was a radio preacher named Brother Muller who would come on for a fifteen-minute radio show. He called himself an evangelist; my Daddy called him a holy-roller preacher. But Daddy always listened to him, and then talked about how stupid he was. But he never missed one of the Brother's shows.

The part I liked best was when Brother Muller would say, *"Now everyone out there in radio land, take one of your handkerchiefs and lay it over the radio. I will pray for your healing."* After his prayer, he would say, *"Now take the handkerchief off the radio and put it over your rheumatism or your headache or whatever else ails you and it will heal your problem."*

He also said, *"If you really want God's Healing Power, then put a five-dollar bill in an envelope and send it to Brother Muller, in care of this station."* He said, *"If you do not have cash, I will take a check, but I prefer cash."*

Finally he announced, *"If you want God's Very Special Healing, you should put your handkerchief in an envelope and send it to Brother Muller, care of this station. I will lay your handkerchief over my own Bible and pray for your healing. But,"* he said, *"Be sure to send a ten-dollar bill and a stamped, self-addressed return envelope so I can send you back your handkerchief for this very special healing."*

My Daddy said, "This is a bunch of hogwash, but if I did have a five-dollar bill, I just might try it." He said, "The only thing that really worries me is that Brother Muller sounds like a nigger man. I would have to see a Kodak picture of Brother Muller before I would send money."

Epilogue

After I finished the eighth grade, my Momma and my older sister, Sue, thought that I should go to a church high school rather than public school. Sue had moved to Madison, Tennessee, near Nashville.

So, when I was fourteen, I left Momma and Daddy in Arkansas to live with Sue and her husband Marvin. Madison Adventist Academy was near their house, so I lived with them and attended high school there and graduated as I had promised my mother.

I was married my senior year of high school. Right after high school, my wife and I moved to a small, rural Adventist-affiliated academy, The Laurel Brook School in the mountains of east Tennessee. The school was self-supported and needed young people to help in the daily running of the institution. We felt needed. There we learned many ways to live on limited means. We had our first child at Laurel Brook, our daughter, Rhonda.

Five years later, as I had also promised my mother, I went to "one of those colleges" she had told me about. My two younger sisters and I were the only of her six kids to finish high school. I was the only one of my siblings to darken a college doorway. While in college, we had our second child, Sheri.

I worked my way through college milking cows, morning and evening, for my first wife's parents on their Oklahoma farm. After completing the bachelor's degree at the University of Oklahoma, I did graduate work in Mexico at The Instituto Allende Art School in San Miguel de Allende, where I completed a Masters of Fine Arts.

Later I taught art at Seventh-day Adventist Colleges in Texas, and in Walla Walla, Washington. I was granted leave and financial support from Walla Walla College to do graduate work towards a doctorate. I completed the Doctorate in Higher Education Administration from Illinois State University. My mother came to my graduation. After the ceremony, she said, "Now, Clydie, since you are now a Doctor, can you write me prescriptions?" I said, "No, Momma, my degree will not let me do that." She looked at me and said, "Now, why would you spend all that time doing a doctor degree and not be able to write a prescription?" I said, "Momma, I don't think I can explain that to you."

After the doctoral program, I taught at the Atlantic Union College in Massachusetts.

I left there, remarried and spent the last twenty years of my art career as the School of Art Director of the Munson Williams Proctor Arts Institute in Utica, New York.

All my siblings are now deceased. My beloved "little brother" Kenny died unexpectedly in 2013.

My wife, Susan, and I went back to my hometown last year to visit. I found the little white wooden church where so much of my young life was spent. It is now a small Spanish-language church. We found the door unlocked. We went inside and things were very much as I remembered. In the back of the church was the large room where we attended church school. The old blackboard was still on the wall, bringing back many fond memories.

We drove out of town to Shady Grove Road and the old home place. It has been a long time since Kenny and I roamed these fields and played in the creeks. All that has changed. The road now has an official name, Longshill Road. The name does not have the charm that Shady Grove does.

The five acres where our little four-room house sat was not recognizable. There are tract houses where my home was, where we flew our kites, where our "secret whisky still" stood and where we built our watermelon stand. Gerard's lake had been drained and a look-alike neighborhood "grew" there.

My beloved sweet gum tree was gone. The only thing I could find to identify my old home place was the ancient hickory tree that stands in what used to be our front yard. My Daddy had whittled whistles for me from its branches. Somehow it escaped the monster bulldozers when they raped our homestead.

I stood under the old tree and wondered if we had a strange privileged upbringing as poor kids that those with more means did not experience. Perhaps poor country people are more primitive, closer to the earth and more base in their thinking, and their actions.

I picked up a hickory nut that had fallen from the hickory tree, and told my wife that I must keep it. It and my memories are all I have left from the home place of *The Boy on Shady Grove Road.*